D0773442

ECONOMICS AND SOCIETY: No. 7

Law and Economics

ECONOMICS AND SOCIETY SERIES
General Editor: Professor C. D. Harbury

NATIONAL UNIVERSITY
LIBRARY
 c₁ 117494

ECONOMICS AND SOCIETY SERIES

Law and Economics
An Introduction

J. M. OLIVER
Head of Economics, Hatfield Polytechnic

London
GEORGE ALLEN & UNWIN
Boston   Sydney

First published in 1979

This book is copyright under the Berne Convention. All rights
are reserved. Apart from any fair dealing for the purpose of
private study, research, criticism or review, as permitted under
the Copyright Act, 1956, no part of this publication may be
reproduced, stored in a retrieval system, or transmitted, in any
form or by any means, electronic, electrical, chemical, mecha-
nical, optical, photocopying, recording or otherwise, without
the prior permission of the copyright owner. Enquiries should
be sent to the publishers at the undermentioned address:

GEORGE ALLEN & UNWIN LTD
40 Museum Street, London WC1A 1LU

© George Allen & Unwin (Publishers) Ltd, 1979

British Library Cataloguing in Publication Data
Oliver, John MacDonald
  Law and economics. — (Economics and society
  series; no.7).
  1. Law — Economics aspects
  I. Title
  340.1'15   K487.E3   79-40680

ISBN 0-04-330297-1
ISBN 0-04-330298-X Pbk

Typeset in 11 on 12 point Times by Red Lion Setters, London
and printed in Great Britain
by Billing & Sons Ltd., Guildford, London and Worcester.

Preface

This short book is designed as an introduction to a field of study which has received little attention in the United Kingdom compared to the United States. Those who wish to read further will have to turn to the pages of the learned journals such as *The Journal of Law and Economics* or *The Journal of Political Economy* or the large American textbooks. I hope that there is enough of interest in this book to stimulate readers to make this effort.

The methodology of an interdisciplinary area such as this always presents problems. The choice of topics and treatment is largely a matter of judgement and I hope that my own preferences are explicit. The focus is that of an economist rather than a lawyer but I have aspired to write for both groups. I have been guided in my choice of topics and treatment by my friends and colleagues Monika Beutel, Ros Levacic, Rhea Martin and Carol Rees, to whom I am grateful. Colin Harbury, the editor of this series, is easily the best editor I have dealt with and readers should be grateful to him. The responsibility for the final outcome is, of course, mine alone.

J. M. OLIVER
Hertford

for Monika

Contents

Introduction

This is an account at an introductory level of some of the features and problems that can be illumined by drawing on both economics and law. The idealised model reader would be a second-year student following courses in both economics and law who had already completed a first-year course in microeconomics.

While it is certainly not a work of original research, I nevertheless hope that it may be of interest to specialist economists because it gives an account of a field of endeavour by economists that has been quite fertile in the United States but of which little notice has yet been taken in the United Kingdom. I hope also that the interest of the material will lighten the penance for economists in reading some quite elementary economics included for other readers.

The book is written for economists and lawyers jointly who are prepared to read at least a little outside their own discipline. When uncertain of how much economics to assume in the reader, I have chosen to err on the side of pessimism and have thus explained rather more than my initial inclination would have led me to do.

Lawyers who have studied no economics whatsoever will, I fear, meet great difficulties, even though I have eliminated all algebra and diagrams and done my best to define the terms as I use them. For the benefit of such lawyers I have indicated some preliminary reading in the bibliographies.

It is not, of course, a text for practising lawyers. The examples chosen and cases discussed meet the needs of the context and do not presume to offer all that a lawyer would need if faced with a technical problem. The cases illustrate the interdependence of law and economics and thus not all the cases are leading cases or specify all the important legal points in that area of the law.

Chapter 1

Law and Economics: Some Inter-Relationships

INTRODUCTION

This book is concerned with the manner in which the law of the land affects economic behaviour and in which economic behaviour generates a need for laws.

One of the purposes of laws is to manoeuvre people into different behaviour patterns to those they would follow in the absence of such laws. Laws may have the explicit purpose of altering economic behaviour and thus have some economic rationale or do so fortuitously, and in both cases economics offers some kind of explanation. It may also be possible not only to understand but also to judge the economic consequences of laws.

Doubtless it would be possible to engage in a grandiose tour of all laws seeking out economic side-effects, but we will confine ourselves to the laws relating to torts, monopolies, information, employment and consumer protection.

Implicit in every law there is a concept of good behaviour consistent with a view of the good society. In a pluralistic society such as the contemporary United Kingdom there is no real consensus on what makes a good society and so there are differing opinions on the law and its operation. Laws alter economic behaviour by forbidding particular acts such as some of the factory legislation or, alternatively, alter the incentives to act in one way rather than another such as the changing doctrines with respect to the specification of negligence.

This means that our first task is to examine the concepts lying behind the idea of 'good' economic behaviour.

Economists have long been preoccupied with the division of labour and one form of their interest has lain in whether they should see themselves as concentrating on narrowly defined problems or, alternatively, as setting few strict limits to their studies.

In recent years the former view has rather held sway, leading to an emphasis on positive economics which tries to model itself on the natural sciences such as physics in three main ways: the precise formulation of hypotheses, the testing of these hypotheses by statistical procedures and resistance to normative statements—that is statements that can only be matters of opinion. This imitative behaviour was once so pervasive that nobody questioned whether or not natural scientists actually proceeded in this manner.

The widespread adoption of positive economics led in its turn to the study of a rather limited set of problems which were amenable to this approach and so economics became identified partly by its method and partly by its content.

Earlier generations of scholars would have found all these developments rather puzzling for they did not specify themselves in this way at all. Adam Smith wrote *The Theory of Moral Sentiments* and gave the *Lectures on Justice, Police, Revenue and Arms* as well as writing *The Wealth of Nations*! Smith thought that there could not be a study of the allocation of scarce resources abstracted from its political and social context. The consequences of a particular economic decision could not be the same all the time and everywhere. John Stuart Mill's main work is entitled *The Principles of Political Economy with some of their applications to Social Philosophy*. Pareto was a sociologist as well as an economist. And so on.

Confining economics to those problems which could be thought of as only economics is strictly a recent development. This rather specialised approach has led to important advances but it has had an unfortunate consequence in that real world problems have an irritating habit of not matching neatly against traditionally defined subjects.

The earlier tradition was lost with the work of Jevons and what is now called neoclassical economics. Briefly, for the moment, this explains how a system of market trading leads simultaneously to one resource allocation, one income distribution and one set of prices from all those that are available. Any redistribution of income leads to a new resource use and any change in resource use leads to a new income distribution. The connection between resource pattern, income distribution and prices is hardly a profound one; Robin Hood's whole purpose in taking from the rich and giving to the poor was to generate greater expenditure by the poor on necessities and less by the rich on luxuries and this would lead to changed prices and so changed outputs, prices and profits. Coupled to this was the claim that this admirable result could be brought about by restricting the role of the government in the economy. Now what the neoclassicists were actually saying was that this desirable result would be achieved, *inter alia*, by perfect competition between many buyers and sellers. It is quite clear that perfect competition is not the norm in those societies which economics sought to illumine so it follows that such economists were actually saying that real world markets did not lead to the best resource use. Those critics who treated economists as though they believed that perfect competition specified the real world were engaged in the well-used debating device of attributing to their opponents what they did not say and then attacking that.

The careful specification of the conditions necessary for optimal resource use made it all too clear that no such result could be brought about autonomously and so the question of a positive economic role for the government did arise. Once there were economic or other reasons for the government to play a positive role, then the interplay between law and economics became clear. The point can be illustrated by a few examples which focus in particular on the interdependence between income distribution and resource allocation.

The United Kingdom legislation on house and flat rentals protects existing tenants so that landlords find it difficult to raise their rents at the same rate as other prices. The tenants are free to cease buying but the landlords are not free to cease selling for the landlords can be held to the contract after its formal terms have lapsed and the economic and social context in which the deal was struck has long changed. This redistributes income from the landlord to the tenant and means that over time landlords simply reduce the supply of accommodation to rent as the opportunities arise. In the long run this simply raises the relative price of rented accommodation available for new leases. Paradoxically, this means that legislation meant to protect the vulnerable—those on short leases—actually penalises the even more vulnerable—those without accommodation at all. This has produced the curious result that the United Kingdom, unlike most European and North American countries, has very little in the way of a market for rented accommodation other than in the tourist and rather expensive sectors. Other countries seem not to have legislated themselves into this impasse and to be quite able to operate a housing market.

A second related example is the Health and Safety at Work Act which may make safety precautions so onerous that the firm actually closes down. It is not unknown for trade unions to oppose the implementation of the Act, apparently revealing a preference for unhealthy, unsafe work over healthy and safe unemployment.

A third, quite different example of the law – economics inter-relationship is the United States specification of negligence in unintentional tort cases which is that the behaviour is negligent if the loss caused by the accident, multiplied by the probability of the accident occurring, exceeds the cost of the precautions that the defendant might have taken to prevent it (*United States v. Carroll Towing Co. (1947)* 159 F2d 169, 2d Cir.)

Not only are economists becoming aware of a rather wider context for their studies than earlier but lawyers too are showing a wider vision: ' . . . it is only when you see the law as a technique of social organisation that you see the problem at all . . . it is the duty of the scholar to search for the social forces that make the law'.[1]

RESOURCE ALLOCATION

The long-surviving problem of economics is to find the best allocation of resources between competing claims as in the allocation of a given field between wheat or barley.

Two aspects are of concern: the specification of the allocation system in different societies and then the appraisal of
the system.

The problems which arise in allocation methods are
essentially those of information. In order to choose
between alternatives, society needs to know just how much
barley would be gained if an area of wheat were forgone—
that is, the opportunity costs of barley and wheat. Society
also needs to know which of the alternatives open to it is
the preferred one and this means resolving the conflict of
interest between those who prefer wheat and those who
prefer barley.

There are a number of ways of coping with these
problems.

1   *Barter Systems*
The method with the least information problem is the
fairly self-sufficient economy in which the farmer simply
specifies his own preference for wheat and barley and
grows amounts consistent with those preferences. In such a
Robinson Crusoe economy the preferred use is directly
known by the farmer and it is scarcely surprising if the
actual use is the preferred use. In such an economy, there is
no market trading and no prices, and the role of the law, if
any, is the enforcement of the dictator's wishes.

Similar features exist within some families which are
coalitions of interests about who should do the gardening
and who the washing-up. Once again, there are no market
prices to allocate one person to one activity and another
person to another and the problem is resolved by some
social bargaining process which might rely on sexist
conventions.

2   *Planned Economics*
The second method, used in large companies and centrally
planned economics such as that of the USSR, allocates
resources in response to prices which are themselves an
indirect message with respect to consumer preferences. The
'prices' are not market prices in the conventional sense but
'shadow' prices generated by planning technique which

attempt to measure the opportunities forgone by a particular production pattern and the preferences placed on various combinations of goods and services. The planning methods thus hope to identify both the production opportunities that are available and the preferred outcome.

Many problems arise in such methods and, in particular, the relationship between prices and ideology is not confined to neoclassical economics. In the USSR, for instance, it is ideologically unacceptable to charge rent for the use of land but land does have an opportunity cost so other ways must be provided of generating the information.

The role of law in such systems is again largely one of monitoring the plan.

3   Market Systems

A third allocative technique, much used in the contemporary Western world, allocates resources between wheat and barley by means of market prices.

Before specifying or appraising such systems, there is a prior question of how market systems came to replace to a large extent barter systems which did offer reasonable prospects that the preferred outcome would be the actual outcome.

Adam Smith had one answer. Simple barter economics of the Robinson Crusoe kind had a low aggregate output because the workers did not specialise and had to attempt a number of quite different tasks each day. If, instead, they were to specialise, then the benefits of the division of labour would be gained and aggregate output would rise leading to higher living standards. As this greater output was won at the expense of self-sufficiency there was a need for exchange.

Exchange through barter had very high transaction and search costs as each individual sought out who wanted what he himself wished to trade and who had what he himself wanted.

Thus specialisation had the twin concomitants of greater output and a need for exchange, and exchange had a lower opportunity cost if it were processed through markets which used prices rather than barter.

Ricardo's answer was rather different and more general, to the effect that individuals had different skills and if each person was allocated to his greatest comparative advantage then it would be to the mutual material benefit of all. Once again there would be specialisation and a need for trade and thus exchange.

There are rather powerful general arguments for trade and for trade through markets but they tell us nothing of how well the market system performs its task.

Specification of Market Trading
Market trading is a deceptively simple system of resource allocation. Starting from some given resource pattern in the society which is being explained, it posits that if that resource use is the optimal one, then market prices will be equilibrium prices. In such an equilibrium, the same quantities will continue to be traded per period at the same prices, so the optimal pattern will be sustained. In other words, *if the actual outcome is the preferred one then equilibrium prices will maintain it.*

If the actual outcome is not the preferred outcome, then disequilibrium prices will lead to a change towards the preferred outcome. If, for instance, society wants more barley and less wheat, then the price of barley will tend to rise and that of wheat will tend to fall. These price changes lead farmers to produce more barley and less wheat because this earns them higher prices at the new set of prices. This new output pattern of barley and wheat simultaneously leads to a new income distribution as the necessary rearrangement of land, labour and capital for barley and wheat was generated by changes in rent, wages and interest. The simultaneity is important; the new resource allocation did not cause the new income distribution nor vice versa.

An important characteristic of this way of thinking is that at equilibrium prices, all markets are cleared—that is, the amount demanded per period is the same as the amount supplied per period at that price. There are thus no sellers at that price who do not find a buyer and no buyers who do not find a seller.

This neat arrangement, represented in textbooks by 'demand and supply' diagrams, shows a system in equilibrium and thus does not represent most real world markets which are clearly in disequilibrium.

Many critics of contemporary economics, including students, seem to believe that neoclassical economists think that such diagrams portray reality. In fact they represent what markets would be like if they were in equilibrium and that is not the same thing at all.

Real world disequilibrium markets manifest quite different characteristics. The quantities supplied per period do not match those demanded per period and consequently stocks rise or fall, queues form or dissatisfied customers turn to different products in different markets. It is the disequilibrium prices which are the very means which reallocate resources into new output patterns which may be the equilibrium markets of the textbooks. This reallocation process is called *tatonnement* and conventional introductory textbooks have remarkably little to say about it. If labour legislation, price controls or some other legal technique prevent or slow down the *tatonnement* process then there are problems to be analysed such as a ranking of the benefits of any such slowing down against the costs.

It is worth noting that a firm which has some discretion over its prices may deliberately charge a non-market clearing price as it may adopt a marketing strategy of 'always leaving them asking for more'. Where this is the case then the whole process of *tatonnement*, which assumes a move towards a market clearing price, fails to occur.

A final warning against misapprehensions gained by unwary students from introductory texts is directed against the idea that equilibrium market prices must be uniquely determined—that is, that there is one price and one price only that will clear the market. In perfectly competitive markets, there is indeed only one such price. In most real world markets, however, such prices may well fall within a range of possibilities. An intuitively understandable example is that in a house sale, the seller might have settled for less and the buyer for more than the actual price. The actual price may not be uniquely determinate but within a range limited by the buyer's top purchase price and the seller's minimum selling price. The market price is then the one that actually exists from within the range that satisfies both parties and the level of the actual price is not explained by economics as normally defined, but by bargaining.

The problem of bargaining with its unpredictable outcome is of interest in our context in plea bargaining, out-of-court settlements, and so forth. The immediate relevance is that such a price is an equilibrium price in the same sense as a perfectly competitive price. The striking difference is that the same amount might have been traded at a higher or lower price. The important difference is that while the same amount might be traded there would be a quite different income distribution at a higher price. The distinction between legal judgements that have a given resource outcome and income distribution and others that have the same resource outcome but a different income distribution will be developed later on.

Before appraising the market system it is worth saying that many people would hold the judgement that the system offered resource allocations independently of the decisions of any one person. This turns out to be only really true in the case of perfect competition but a number of markets do have some of the characteristics of an autonomous system in which no single buyer or seller has a dominant role. And what is more, transaction costs are minimised.

Appraisal of the Market System
It is not in fact a criticism of textbooks that the real world is in a process of adjustment rather than in a state of equilibrium. This is because the adjustment process can only be understood by reference to the idea of an equilibrium for it is the latter idea that specifies why adjustment may be necessary and how the problem might be resolved. The equilibrium concept does not describe reality but it may help us to interpret reality.

It is important to separate criticism of the market trading model from criticism of market trading as an allocation device. The model is of limited applicability because many resource decisions are taken without reference to prices because they are taken inside large companies. Such bodies respond to factors other than prices when they allocate factors to geriatric clinics rather than child clinics or to one model of a car rather than another. A further limit on the applicability of the model is the assumption that buyers and sellers respond to price changes by seeking out the most profitable output, or the highest wage or the lowest price. Higher profits may mean less leisure, higher wages may mean worse working conditions and the time and effort of finding the new employment and seeking out the lowest price means bearing higher transaction and search costs. It is thus possible for changes in prices not to imply changes in economic behaviour.

Quite different in nature is the critique, not of the model, but of market systems as an allocation method. The attack focuses on whether market prices actually show the production possibilities available and which of them is the preferred outcome. In so far as the market does respond to price signals, the question arises of whether the signals are accurate information.

If, at the margin, an economy can produce three tons of wheat for every ton of barley forgone then the prices need to be in the ratio £3 per ton of barley to £1 per ton of wheat. At any other price ratio, the money costs will not correspond to the real costs and the goods will seem cheaper than they really are in terms of alternative production forgone. The consumer, perceiving these bogus prices, then makes misinformed decisions. In a similar manner, a colour-blind person perceives wrong colours and thus chooses an unfortunate decor.

There are a number of reasons for believing that market prices seldom correspond to real opportunity costs.

First, monopolies generate prices that exceed opportunity costs. This is true of both input and product markets and labour and monopoly legislation is one of the most common areas of joint concern to both economists and lawyers.

Externalities are a second source of market failure in that they produce a divergence between private and social costs and benefits. The best-known examples in the contemporary world are pollution and noise nuisance in which one party generates costs for the other and the second party may have no contractual right to compensation. The law of torts can be relevant in this case.

Thirdly, the consumer cannot know the real costs of a good or service which has no market price, such as defence and police systems and many forms of health and education. In such cases, the role of the law seems to be restricted to monitoring the standards of service (medical negligence suits) or their use by the public (parking offences). The most common term for such instances is 'collective consumption goods'.

All these problems relate to decisions taken in a world of inadequate information. A further problem is that the process of price formation may itself be on the basis of incomplete information. Buyers and sellers may have quite unequal information with respect to their relative bargaining positions. Much contemporary consumer protection legislation, for instance, is designed to redress the balance between shopkeepers and their suppliers on the one hand and the customers on the other. Legislation designed to make companies publish more information in their accounts performs a similar role with respect to the bargaining positions of firms and trade unions. Such legislation might well affect the *tatonnement* process and so the eventual outcome with respect to prices, resource allocations and income distributions.

RESOURCE ALLOCATION CRITERIA

The criteria that help us to rank alternative resource allocations are a good advertisement for the ingenuity of economists. In the present context, only two are necessary. The equi-marginal returns rule and the related Pareto criterion help us to eliminate some possibilities, and the second best theorem and compensation tests will enable further progress.

The Equi-Marginal Returns Rule

Equi-marginal returns is a deceptively simple rule that resources should be allocated between alternatives so that marginal returns are equal in all uses. Whenever marginal returns are unequal, then obviously resources should be allocated to the higher-yielding activity and away from the other and this process should be continued until such worthwhile transfers are no longer possible. This equilibrium position is reached when the marginal returns are equal in all uses so that the equalisation of marginal returns is the optimising technique.

This is clear and straightforward in theory but rather difficult in practice. The problems become all too apparent if we apply this counsel of perfection to the criminal justice system which is a topic of interest to both lawyers and economists.

An early problem is to define the optimal level of offences and the related ideas of the optimal level of punishment and the optimal combinations of punishment. It might seem that the optimal level of offences is zero but this is hardly the case if the last offence prevented is a parking offence and if the resources needed to prevent it have a very high value in some alternative use.

Once it is clear that the optimal level of offences is not likely to be zero then a rational enforcement policy requires that level and combination of penalties where the *marginal damage to society of the last offence shall equal the marginal cost to society of prevention*. This is, of course, simply an application of the equi-marginal rule.

Some difficulties are immediately apparent. Some forms of punishment, like capital punishment, are hardly open to the marginal approach. Indeed, such a penal policy may make the criminal commit more offences in order to avoid detection. Further, for some offences, the optimal fine may be so high that it cannot be collected.

In any case, there is hardly a tariff matching crimes against punishments—although there are, of course, both conventional and maximum penalties for most crimes. There is no strict tariff as consideration must be given to past and likely future offences. This implies that for a given offence a fine may be the appropriate policy for one offender and a jail sentence for another.

If the first difficulty is the restricted applicability of penal policy to marginal adjustment, the second is the difficulty of measuring the 'output' of the criminal justice system. The output might be 'measured' in arrests, convictions or preventions (the difference between actual and predicted crime).

As we choose different objective(s) for the criminal justice system, so we get different 'correct' resource allocations of, say, police manpower between motor-cycle patrols and detective squads. In this context, a 'correct' allocation is simply one consistent with a given objective. It is a normative matter to choose an objective for the criminal justice system and it is not straightforward in a pluralist society.

It is perfectly possible for the criminal justice system to be multi rather than single objective in nature. No doubt the police would like to minimise the number of crimes committed and maximise the arrests for those crimes that are committed; but the point is that to improve performance in one respect is to hazard it with respect to the other goal.

A further problem is that in 'measuring' crime we are concerned not only with the number of crimes but also with their seriousness. We are in immediate difficulties if we try to measure output by 'market value'. We are in difficulty if we equate ten thefts of £100 with one theft of £1,000 but we are also in difficulty if we say that one is greater than the other. In practice, the police allocate their efforts between petty and serious crimes in response to local political and social pressures and the problem is compounded by the fact that much crime, especially petty crime, goes unreported to the police.

Once some necessarily arbitrary decision has been taken on the objectives of police efforts, there is a further problem in measuring police output in that most crimes are committed by those who already have a criminal record which helps the detection rate for some crimes. A more important dimension of the problem is that this means that we should not look at, say, the arrests record by itself for this depends on the efficacy of other parts of the criminal justice system such as the prison and probation services; and, of course, vice versa, as one cannot reform a criminal who has not been identified by the police. It is a policy of sub-optimisation to concentrate only on one part of the system such as the police; it is preferable to optimise over the whole system and this includes the downstream costs such as the prison service.

A related problem is that if police activity in one year changes criminal activity in a succeeding year then those costs and benefits cannot be directly compared and the future money sums must be discounted to present values.

The whole idea of measuring the economic value of crimes to be compared with the economic value of social resources is a necessary exercise but it is a conceptual minefield. The *cost to the criminal* is the foregone legitimate earnings during the planning and commission of the crime. This helps to explain crime rates among the poor, for in this sense they have little to lose. This cost should be adjusted by an imputed value for any emotion that the criminal experiences, such as fear or elation. The *benefit to the criminal* is the expected monetary gain rather than the actual outcome—again adjusted for any emotion. Where the criminal has good information about the contents of a house he intends to rob and a clear idea of the price he can expect on disposing of the goods, then this expected monetary gain can be reasonably estimated. There is, however, a class of crimes such as sex offences where the expected monetary gain is not easily estimated other than as that sum the criminal would pay in order to commit the crime which is not normally a figure to which there is access.

The *cost to the victim* is the direct money losses. These may easily be established in most theft cases and it is the second-hand price he would have gained if he had tried to sell the goods and not what he has to pay to replace them. The victim's loss does, of course, need to be adjusted to take account of any psychological effects of the crime upon him. For the same reason that it is difficult to assess the expected monetary gain of crimes such as an assault upon the police, it is also problematic to value some costs to the victim such as lost health or life. The particular form of the problem—that there is no market comparable to the market for stolen jewellery—will be discussed later.

The *cost to society*, other than those to the criminal and the victim, is the resources of the criminal justice system in the police, court and penal service that it provides. Some of these resources such as police cars have a clear market value while others, such as the forgone production represented by the juror's time, can only be imputed.

These difficulties of measurement and of marginal adjustments mean that while the equi-marginal returns rule is useful and helpful it is of limited applicability in practice. Many non-economists would offer further criticisms of this whole approach in that it assumes rationality in the criminal; this point has little or no weight as we could make no progress by assuming criminal behaviour was random as such behaviour clearly does show patterns. A further criticism of this kind of decision theory approach is that in deciding the penalty it ignores other factors such as vengeance, a custodial role for the recidivist and criminally insane or simply 'pour décourager les autres'.

It should be said that this approach to analysing the problems does give some insights. Concurrent sentences may encourage crime as they reduce the cost to the criminal of each crime. Habitual crime may be partly explained by the lack of employment opportunities and it becomes understandable that eighteenth-century capital punishment for sheep stealing did not deter the poor. An enforcement agency choosing at the margin between increasing the probability of detection or the penalty may well find that the latter is the cheaper method of gaining a given change in the level of the offence. It may be very difficult to increase the detections for a crime such as salmon poaching so it may be cheaper to manoeuvre a criminal who accepts a given probability of conviction and a given penalty into changing his behaviour by altering the penalty rather than the probability of detection. Indeed, it may be that the most sensible method of measuring police output is not by convictions or preventions but by the costs and benefits of changing the level of offence.

The Pareto Criterion

Related to the equi-marginal rule is the Pareto criterion, which holds that one situation is unambiguously better than another if, and only if, the change to the first situation benefits at least one person and does not harm any other. *All such improvements should be made and the resultant resource allocations are Pareto efficient.*

The Second Best Theorem

While the equi-marginal rule is attractive there is an important difficulty even in those circumstances where it is a practical proposition. Many quite different resource allocations (and thus income distributions) may all be Pareto efficient. Two important points follow from the fact that the equi-marginal rule eliminates some outcomes but does not produce a unique outcome. Every time the Pareto criterion is used to select a resource use a decision is simultaneously made with respect to income distribution, simply because every set of prices has an income distribution and a resource use consistent with it. Further, to make a decision with respect to one Pareto outcome is to make a 'second best' decision. The second best theorem holds that, in a complex world, to make one part of the economy Pareto efficient is not necessarily to make the entire economy better off.[2]

These principles mean that a judge who gives an award for damages is not only fixing a price but simultaneously affecting incomes and resources. They also mean that if courts rid society of a monopoly the decision needs justification in terms other than simply that monopoly is Pareto inefficient.

The Compensation Test

This is one way of coping with these problems. In its simplest form it holds that if the gainers in a new situation receive sufficient benefit to compensate the losers, and after the compensation is paid the losers will not have lost their original welfare level, then that is a reason for choosing the new situation. Similarly, if the losers in the proposed new outcome are able to compensate the potential gainers so that they forgo their gains, then that is a reason for choosing the present situation. It is a quite separate matter whether any compensation is paid, for the criterion is that the size of the potential gain in welfare is greater than the potential loss.

This approach is clearly related to the Pareto criterion and will be used cautiously in Chapter 2. It has created a complex literature in economics but all that now need be said is that it holds both that money has a constant marginal utility and that it is possible to make interpersonal comparisons of utility. Both these propositions are unsound and will be discussed in later chapters. The point may be grasped intuitively by considering whether the richest man in the world should be allowed to pay motorists to make a detour rather than drive past his house. Few would argue that the fact he was willing to do so meant that the economic welfare he lost necessarily exceeded that lost by the motorists in having to make the detour. Such a conclusion fails because it assumes that a given sum of money means the same to rich and poor.

Some understanding of the simultaneity of income distribution, resource allocation and prices and of the applicability of the Pareto and compensation tests may be gained from the following examples. In cases where courts award fines or damages they not only affect resource allocations by changing the behaviour of potential defendants but they also generate an income distribution different from that which would otherwise have occurred. The deterred criminal remains poor, the person who would otherwise have been a victim remains rich, and the party who would otherwise have been negligent now incurs the costs of greater care. In the bargaining situation mentioned earlier, in which one price occurs from a range of possible prices, there are implications for out-of-court settlements. If the court's expected decision in an insurance case is between that for which the plaintiff would settle out of court and that for which the insurance company would settle then it is possible for both parties to reach a Pareto-efficient out-of-court settlement better than their own initial positions and possibly with a much lower transaction cost. They may 'trade' in court because at least one of the parties believes that he would do better in court than in a prior settlement. Such a belief may, of course, have been falsified.

Earlier it was said that concurrent sentencing was not part of a rational enforcement policy but it may be explained in the light of the 'trading' implicit in plea bargaining. The criminal confesses to a number of crimes where the chances of conviction are low in return for expectations of concurrent or lenient sentencing. The police have gained convictions that would otherwise have been impossible to gain or at the best with very high transaction costs. In the trading exchange the police accept the certainty of conviction and probability of minor sentences for the uncertainty of a possibly higher sentence and the criminal makes the reverse exchange.

Many real world trades of a more conventional nature are of this kind, with the buyer and seller knowing that they might have done better or worse but uncertain of the outcome. In perfect competition, of course, there is a determinate price and no problem of this kind.

This is part of the economic rationale behind contracts and contract law which both make possible and sustain trading at certain prices when less or no trading would otherwise occur. Contracts also free the parties from the transactions costs of constant renegotiating and they are part of the *tatonnement* process which maximises the possibilities of advantageous trade.

Property rights also take on a new role when seen in this light. Property rights are one of the incentives of efficient resource use; if there are no property rights but common rights, then economic behaviour takes on a new form. The common grazing rights of the American West led to overgrazing until the land was fenced in and property rights were assigned. There is a similar rationale behind the continual extension of national fishing rights to limit the overfishing that occurs in international waters.

It will be evident that 'prices' is one of the techniques for moving resources from one activity to another, such as crime or trespass, and prices thus present a way in which the community might attempt to influence the level of activity. The 'prices', may be conventional market prices or court decisions. And a court decision involving a gaol sentence involves opportunity costs to society and the prisoner and thus it is as much a 'price' as a fine.

NOTES

1 O. Kahn-Freund, 'The legal framework of society', in *Man and the Social Sciences*, ed. W. A. Robson (London: Allen & Unwin, 1975).
2 R. G. Lipsey and K. J. Lancaster, 'The general theory of the second best', *Review of Economic Studies* (1957).

BIBLIOGRAPHY

Good introductory books in microeconomics are:
G. Hewitt, *Economics of the Market* (London: Fontana, 1976);
R. Dorfman, *The Price System* (Englewood Cliffs, NJ: Prentice-Hall, 1964).

Chapter 2

Property Rights, Externalities and Torts

INTRODUCTION

A study of the economic aspects of torts illustrates some of the benefits of applying economic principles to legal processes and also some of the limitations of economics.

Economics has great strength in identifying equilibrium resource uses but is rather weaker in specifying the adjustment process as society moves from one equilibrium to another. It also becomes necessary to emphasise the social origin of many economic problems rather more than do some of the technical economic texts.

A useful starting-point is that trading exchanges in a market presuppose 'contracts' which may be explicit in written documents, which may be implicit in statute law[1] or which may take the looser forms of reasonable expectations.

For present purposes, torts come into play either when such contracts do not exist or when they are ineffective—that is, torts operate largely where one or both parties to an exchange are dissatisfied and can find no remedy in a contract action. If a worker, for instance, serving a contract of employment was injured while at work, then if he could get no redress by suing for breach of his contract of employment he might succeed in a tort action for negligence.

Linked to the concept of contract is the concept of property rights which may be either an obligation which one party has to another and which would be sustained by the courts or a reasonable expectation which one party has of another. The former is clearly a special case of the latter where the reasonable expectations are supported by the legal system. A person working for a firm has a right in the first sense to be paid his salary in the manner specified and the courts would support him, but a worker for a city centre firm has no property right that the firm must provide him with free parking, although they may assign such a property right to favoured employees.

Externalities focus on the notion that one party may be excluded from charging for all the benefits he has created for others or from paying for all the costs for which he is responsible. If one farmer lawfully pollutes a river in such a manner that a farmer downstream faces increased costs for a given level of output then that is an external cost, while if he had discharged cleaner water it would be an external benefit. Society can, in principle, cope with these problems in a number of ways.

Taxes or subsidies may be imposed so that the first farmer now faces costs that do measure all the costs and benefits for which he is responsible. An alternative technique is to impose restrictions of a quantitative nature which limit the level of the activity which is operating as an externality—smokeless fuels and emission consents are examples of this kind of quantitative restriction. The economic effect, of course, is to place the cost squarely on those responsible for creation of the effect. A further method of 'internalising' the externality is by merging the two firms into one. A farmer who pollutes a lake in which there is commercial fishing is generating an externality on others only if the fishing rights are held by others. If he has the fishing rights then its his own assets which he puts at hazard. The significance of property rights will be explored later.

Externalities are not simply a minor curiosity of life. Their significance is the manner in which their existence distorts money prices so that they fail to indicate the true cost of production or the true benefits, as the case may be. This means that the consumer is more innocent than he need be and in consequence may choose an output combination other than the best available. In the hypothetical example below, marginal private and social benefits are the values of extra crops grown as the result of weedkiller and the private benefits to the farmer are the same as those to society which enjoys the extra production. Private costs are the money costs for the gallons of weedkiller paid by the farmer who simply follows the equi-marginal returns rule and uses 4 gallons. Society would prefer that he uses 3 gallons for it addresses itself to the marginal social costs which is the private costs plus the cost of the externality which in this case might be forgone fishing.

Gallons of weedkiller	1	2	3	4	5
Marginal social and private benefits	10	9	8*	7*	6
Marginal private costs	7	7	7	7*	7
Marginal social costs	6	7	8*	9	10

In these circumstances, decisions based on money prices lead to a resource use other than the preferred one essentially because of information failures. External costs lead to industries operating at too high a level and external benefits to the industry responsible for the phenomenon operating at too low a level.

Other than the techniques already mentioned, a further possible method of dealing with externalities is the tort action. Economists have taken little interest in this feature although they have been interested in bargaining which is a likely feature of tort actions. The possibilities can be seen quickly enough with two examples.

There is in some circumstances in English law a 'right to lights' and this is a property right in both senses of a reasonable expectation and one which will be supported by the courts. This means that the owner of a property already in existence who lost natural light into his property because another building was erected would have a right to compensation or for the later building to be demolished. In fact the operation of United Kingdom planning laws are likely to prevent any such outcome but the interdependence between the externality, property rights and torts is clear enough.

A second instructive example is *US* v. *Causby* (1948) USSC 221, in which a North Carolina chicken farmer successfully sued an airport. Noisy landings were reducing the egg-laying performances of his birds and the US

Supreme Court held that his 'property' had been taken contrary to the US Constitution Fifth Amendment.

This widens the definition of 'property' beyond that of physical property to include the 'characteristics' of the physical asset. This wider definition is attractive to economists and pre-dates modern work on demand theory which in fact focuses on the characteristics of a good rather than the good itself.[2]

The potential in tort actions for coping with externalities is now obvious. The plane landings generate the externality and the farmer seeks redress in the courts. If he is successful either the plane landings are reduced or he receives financial compensation which, if it returns him to his original position or better, is Pareto efficient. If the landing schedules are changed, the the court has provoked a different resource allocation in real terms and a different income distribution. If the airport is willing to pay enough to maintain landings and also return him to his original income position or better then both parties have traded in court to a better position than before—although from the airport's viewpoint not as good a position as if the case had not been brought. Such an outcome is Pareto efficient relative to the pre-tort position but has a different income distribution from that corresponding to the period after the tort but before the case was brought. This intervening position was not Pareto efficient relative to the pre-tort position in that, compared with earlier, the airport was better off but the farmer worse.

Before we take this or other cases any further, it is important to seek out the link between externalities and property rights.

Returning to the first example, if the upstream farmer *has the right* to discharge polluted water and the downstream farmer has to incur purification costs attributable to the first farmer's production activities, then the first has imposed a cost, that is an externality, on the second. If the downstream farmer *has the right* to unpolluted water and the upstream farmer has to intall purification plant only because the other farmer exists then it is the latter who imposes an externality on the former. *The assignment of the externalities depends on the prior assignments of the property rights.*

When Pigou and other neoclassical economists first discussed externalities, little or no attention was paid to this aspect. Discussions took place about vehicles turning right across traffic and making the oncoming traffic slow down without it always being made explicit that to identify the externality in this way necessarily attributed a right to one party and not the other. A 'No Right Turn' sign which forced the first set of drivers to make a detour and allowed the second group to proceed normally reversed which party imposed an externality on the other.

This raises the prior question of the distribution of property rights which in the present context will simply be taken as given.

Two earlier comments now make more sense.

If an externality is 'internalised' by merging two firms, such as our original two farms, then the property rights are assigned in such a way that the farmer's discharge of polluted water now imposes a cost on himself and he will certainly now address himself to all costs in following the equi-marginal rule.

The market prices will be correct measures of real costs, at least with respect to externalities, when the property relationships are consistent with the economic relationships expressed in the costs. It is when one firm, in the course of its own production, can impose a cost on another that the property rights relationships do not correspond to economic reality and the market prices fail to measure the real costs of alternatives forgone.

Economists' discussions on these problems have contrasted the 'polluter pays' principle in which the first farmer compensates the second farmer for polluting the watercourse with the 'pollutee pays' principle in which the second farmer pays the first not to pollute the water. The choice of one or other of these methods is in effect an assignment of property rights. The former seems to be the more common which simply says that the law tends to sustain the position that has become historically established. Generally, those whose property has always enjoyed a pollution-free watercourse will do well in court and those who buy property in an area with a well-established chemical industry will get short shrift if they go to court demanding that others change their behaviour so that they may themselves start to enjoy fishing.

There are examples of the 'pollutee pays' principle. The Crown Estate Commissioners, who own Windsor Great Park, and Berkshire County Council, which contains the park, paid the organisers of a pop festival in 1975 provided that the festival was held elsewhere.[3] The principle is also present in some out-of-court settlements where one party in effect 'pays' the other not to take the matter to court by, for instance, the polluted farmer settling for a certain but lower sum in the present rather than a higher but uncertain sum in the future.

It will be clear that the choice of one of these principles over the other affects the outcome, as they do not always lead to the same result.

The sum of money which the chicken farmer must be paid to allow the planes to land which will return him to his original position with respect to income need not equal the minimum sum which the airport would pay in order to continue operation. According to the principle followed, and so the sum awarded, the outcome will differ with respect both to income distribution and to resource allocation.

Some of the earliest work on these problems[4] suggested that in fact the court settlement was irrelevant to the outcome for the market would always produce the 'best' solution if the court had failed to do so.

A leading case, much quoted by economists, was *Sturgess* v. *Bridgeman*.[5] The facts were that a doctor was unable to use his newly built surgery extension due to noise from the machinery in a neighbouring confectioner. The court upheld his claim, imposing an injunction on the confectioner.

One attitude is that all this is irrelevant as the market will operate to produce the result that the community requires. Assume that the use of his premises to the doctor is worth £80 per week and the use to the confectioner of his premises is worth £100 per week. If the doctor gains the injunction then the confectioner will pay him more than £80 per week for a release and thus it is the highest value resource use which prevails.

A first problem is that there is an assumption that the market prices do indicate the true extent of costs and benefits. As it is the market prices that cause the resource misallocation in the first place, it is rather anomalous to use them to manoeuvre society to a correct allocation.

A second difficulty is that there is little evidence that such markets are in operation save when the sums of money are very great. Such markets would only exist if there were zero transaction costs or if the litigation costs, including the transaction costs, were expected to be less than the loss of accepting the injunction. Finally such a market would only exist in those cases where injunctions were used by the court for there would be no such trading process if the doctor were awarded £150 in damages. It is feasible to buy off an injunction for up to £100 but is rather unusual to buy £150 for £100.

A more fruitful approach is to recognise three conditions which must be met before the world is free of this sort of problem.[6] Property rights must be properly defined and assigned; where there are differences of opinion about these property rights then the litigation costs must be less than the externality costs and the transaction costs in any post-court market must be less than the externality costs.

Since none of these conditions, let alone all three, is consistently met in the real world, we can be sure that there are problems to be illumined.

It is helpful to organise the discussion into five separate but related issues. Who pays in the event of an externality being resolved in a tort action? In what circumstances does he pay? What 'prices' are used to 'value' the externality? How far do the economists' and lawyers' approaches to these problems conflict and coincide? What light do these discussions throw on the growing practice of strict liability?

WHO IS LIABLE IN A TORT ACTION CONCERNING AN EXTERNALITY?

As was hinted earlier, conventional economics discusses alternative techniques for dealing with the problem once it has been decided which party is imposing the externality on the other. There is no criterion in economics which will answer this prior question. Economists normally take this answer as given by accepting the existing distribution of historically determined property rights.

There is an attractive pragmatism about analysing the world as it is but there is an hidden assumption that the pre-tort position and resource allocation is the 'correct' one and that the burden of proof is on those who wish to make changes in it.

There is nothing in positive economics to support this attitude and in fact a different presumption will hold that both the pre-tort and post-court allocations are likely to be sub-optimal. A ranking of a scientific nature of these two sub-optimal allocations is unlikely unless a great deal more information is available than is commonly the case, so that if the court chooses one sub-optimal outcome rather than another it must be engaged in a social judgement. We would expect, and perhaps hope, that these social judgements by the court correspond to generally held social opinions. In this light, the practice of taking the pre-tort position as the norm and taking existing distributions of property rights as given is consistent with a generally held acceptance of the market system.[7] There is no doubt that in loose terms the legal system sustains the existing social framework. This sometimes enrages radical critics but it is really no more surprising that Western laws support capitalism than that ecclesiastical law is consistent with the view of the world taken by the Church of England.

IN WHAT CIRCUMSTANCES DOES THE PARTY RESPONSIBLE FOR THE EXTERNALITY LOSE A TORT ACTION?

In the present context, it is assumed that the alternative

techniques available, such as taxes, mergers and quantitative restrictions, are not in use and that a tort action has been brought. The discussion is also restricted to those torts that might correspond to an externality and not those torts that correspond to other sources of non-optimal prices such as monopolies or torts such as assault and battery which have economic consequences but no apparent effect on prices.

The economist would be anxious to see a person responsible for an externality lose a tort action in all cases where his behaviour distorted prices and so the resource use. The lawyer approaches the problem of economic loss or benefit caused by one party with respect to another in a quite different manner using a different set of concepts.

The initial position is quite straightforward. *There is no general liability for economic loss in tort.*[8] This attitude is understandable, if not particularly supportable, once the law is seen as supporting the contemporary social system. The market system is based on competition so that if one greengrocer drove another bankrupt by his superior trading skills there would be no recompense in law. All competitions have to have losers and it is difficult to safeguard the losers without overturning the system.

The absence of a general liability for economic loss has slowly become unworkable as society has grown more complex, as our economic interdependence has become more marked and as political and social confidence in the market system has become more uncertain. In response to these developments the general rule of no liability for economic loss has remained but a number of special cases are allowed. In general these categories match circumstances in which it is felt that the economic loss is not due to the operation of a competitive market system but some other factor such as 'unfair trading practices'.

The lawyer's categorisation is quite different from that of the economist although clearly sometimes externality is dealt with by lawyers perfectly well but not because they see it as an externality.

The lawyer's classification of economic torts[9] is:

1   Loss caused by means intrinsically legal such as some
    forms of inducing breach of contract;
2   loss caused by illegal means such as intimidation;
3   loss caused by injurious falsehood such as passing-off.

Some of these will be dealt with later in chapters on
monopoly and information and the present focus will be
mainly on torts, economic loss and externalities.

It is clear that if one greengrocer inflicted loss on
another due to his competitive trading expertise then the
second greengrocer would have no remedy in court. The
kind of exception that has attracted lawyers is where the
economic loss could be attributed to the *fault* of the first
shopkeeper. As we shall see later the development of 'strict
liability' is weakening this criterion but it remains true that
fault liability has been the main theme of United Kingdom
law in this area.

The concentration on fault is quite alien to the economist's way of thinking which has been quite content with
the fact of an externality and finds no need to apportion
blame.

The general legal attitude has been that if one greengrocer in the course of his work caused a genuinely
accidental outbreak of disease in his spoilage which
damaged the stocks of his neighbouring greengrocer then
the second would be in a weak, but not impossible, position in a court action. If the outbreak were due to *negligence* then the victim would be in a much stronger position. The criteria used by judges in awarding damages for
economic loss which by implication are not the result of a
competitive market system are:

1   conspiracy;
2   negligence;
3   intention;
4   overt act.

These clearly reflect social judgements and priorities as
they are perceived by the judges and they are quite inde-
pendent of any perception about resource allocation or

indeed any underlying theme for torts developed in response to particular problems and then lay where they fell.

A clear difference between the economist's approach and that of the lawyer is that traditional torts were concerned with physical injury but the economist has no difficulty in seeing economic loss where there is no tangible effect. Unless the loss were the result of criminal acts the law has been reluctant to see the concept of damage extended to non-physical forms. Implicit in any such development is a re-definition of 'property' to include its characteristics in the mode of thinking in the *US* v. *Causby* case. United Kingdom practice is becoming more flexible so that, for instance, it is now more common than it once was not only for the owners of property knocked down for a new motorway route to be compensated but also those who maintain their physical asset but lose some of its characteristics such as peace and quiet.

There are three reasons why the law has been slow to correspond to the economist's way of thinking in this respect and even now it happens only in a rather piecemeal fashion.

First, judges frequently like to present themselves as personally uninvolved and neutral and this is much easier when the damage is physically measurable and especially so when there is a 'market' in which it can be directly 'valued' by a builder's bill for repairs.

A second reason is a 'floodgates of litigation' argument which takes the view that once we allow one case there is no way of knowing where it will all end. The argument is less than persuasive—for, if the litigation floodgates were open, that very fact should decrease the level of actionable behaviour.

A third connected reason why lawyers like to restrict themselves to the world of physical property and its damage is shown in the case of *Weller & Co.* v. *National Foot and Mouth Disease Research Institute*.[10] The facts of the case were that the plaintiffs were auctioneers who lost profits due to the cancellation of auctions after an outbreak of the disease caused by the negligence of the defendants.

The farmers whose cattle died or were destroyed had lost a physical asset and they were compensated, but the defendants resisted paying the auctioneers and the court supported them in their resistance. The lawyers were really making two distinctions: the farmers had lost both a physical asset and a reasonable expectation of profits while the auctioneers had lost only the latter. In terms of economic loss caused by the defendants' negligence there is small distinction between the two cases. However the lawyer also makes a distinction on the question of 'remoteness'. The argument is that the auctioneers' claim and interest was too remote and that, if it were allowed, there could also be a good claim by a lady who gained extra part-time work as a barmaid on the days the auctions were held. It seems a little hard on plaintiffs that they should lose their claim because otherwise others would win theirs. In any event, the question is one of drawing a sensible line in remoteness and the size of transactions costs would soon be greater than the size of the loss in the more remote cases.

The emphasis of the law on property in its tangible form has been well summed up: 'The Courts *never* deny compensation for a physical takeover . . . [even if] the invasion is practically trifling from the owner's point of view; a marginally encroaching sidewalk for example.'[11]

One final distinction remains to be made in the partial correspondence between the economist's treatment of the externality problem and the lawyer's. *There is no parallel between the external benefit and torts.* If one good shop attracts more trade to a street and so others benefit, the first party has no claim in law to the extra profits of the second parties. This is hardly surprising because the very word 'tort' means 'wrong' and the law has been concerned with unfortunate victims of the competitive system rather than those who have gained fortunate benefits.

WHICH 'PRICES' SHOULD BE USED IN 'VALUING' ECONOMIC LOSS?

As in all pricing problems, the courts should use prices that are consistent with their objectives. The prices that will return the plaintiff to his original position need not be the same as those that would change the defendant's behaviour. The court must decide what it wishes to do and then choose the appropriate prices.

If the intention is to return the plaintiff to his original pre-tort position then a sum should be awarded that puts him in the same position in the market—that is, that he will be able to buy the same goods and services that he would have enjoyed if the tort had not occurred. If he is awarded a sum to replace the income that he would have earned from his lost shop or other asset then a stock of money is replacing a flow. It must be realised that he has lost an asset (which might be his health, a cowherd or a factory) and the income that that asset would have generated.

Strictly, the lost profits on a shop worth a given sum need not be the same as for other shops worth the same sum and no doubt the courts would have to restrict themselves to some crude rule-of-thumb which might be average profits or even the interest rate. All rules-of-thumb produce crude results but all rules-of-thumb have low transaction costs.

To return him to his original position in the market, the figure should also be adjusted for any inflation and the retail price index might serve as a further crude decision rule which would minimise the transaction costs of all settlements in aggregate, even if some plaintiffs had lost production the market prices of which had risen at a faster or slower rate than the index.

In all cases market prices would have to be used with a great deal of care. To take a simple example, it is quite possible that the market price of cattle might be altered by the very fact that the plaintiff who was unable to bring his cattle to market produced a large proportion of the normal supplies.

A more pressing difficulty is when the lost production is partly in the non-market sector, for it then becomes necessary to 'impute' a price which 'values' the lost peace and quiet or whatever. Rough and ready methods are available in the price changes of a house following the building of a motorway; such changes tell us how the market values the lost peace and quiet and the better transport routes and not how the particular individual does. In other, more difficult cases such as lost health or family life, any such imputed prices can be little more than an act of judgement although the economist can make them an act of informed judgement.

Problems also arise when the tort occurred in another country and the sum awarded is expressed in the currency of that other country. Fluctuations in the international exchange rates can have marked effects on the plaintiff's position in the market when the money is transferred to his own currency. In the EEC, many awards, especially in insurance cases, are expressed in European units of account (1EUA = £0.08) which means that sums awarded in courts other than the country of domicile have a known meaning in the domestic currency. A certain sum is thus gained in exchange for an uncertain sum that might have been higher or lower. This device does not, of course, protect the plaintiff from different rates of inflation in the two currencies.

A further set of problems arises if the plaintiff has acted in the market other than to maximise his money income. A worker, for instance, might work four days a week in order to free himself to go fishing. In any such case, he values the non-market activity of leisurely fishing higher than the money income of an extra day's work a week. A problem arises if such a person is injured in such a manner that he is unable to work again. Should he be awarded a sum equal to what he in fact chose to earn or to what he might have earned? There are no clear legal precedents at the moment but the economist would favour one sum for the lost income and another for the lost leisure which must at least equal a day's pay as his behaviour reveals that he prefers the leisure to the pay. As he was willing to 'trade' a day's pay then that is at least what the fishing was worth to him.

An analogous problem arises if the plaintiff has lost a wife who was in fact earning and who, as a result of an accident, has to be replaced in the home by a housekeeper. Should the husband be awarded what his wife would have earned or what he has to pay the housekeeper? The former is a market valuation of his wife's professional skills and the latter is the market price of her housewifely skills. In many cases there might not be too much difference, but it is a serious problem if his wife happens to have been an international opera star.

There are also in such cases the problems of non-market losses such as the happiness of family life. It is difficult to see how a price could possibly be imputed for such a loss, although Scottish law allows a 'solatium' payment which is seen, not as measuring the loss in money terms, but as a gesture of sympathy. The sum is normally small. Damage to sexual enjoyment due to physical injuries is recognised by the courts just like any other physical injury and rather arbitrarily determined sums are awarded.

If the courts were not concerned with returning the plaintiff to his pre-tort position but with awarding sums that reflect the real costs in alternatives forgone and real benefits then they would, of course, exchange the problems of market prices for those met in cost-benefit analysis.[12] So far, this is a sophistry with which the courts have not concerned themselves.

The economist would favour this latter approach if the objective of the courts was not to return to something like the original position but to achieve a different outcome, particularly with respect to resource allocation.

CONFLICT AND COINCIDENCE IN THE LAWYER'S AND ECONOMIST'S APPROACH

It will be clear by now that torts refer to problems other than externalities and that not all externalities have torts corresponding to them. Those tort actions which do correspond to externalities offer a perfectly feasible method of coping with the problem but so far it has been rather under-used compared with other techniques. It should be emphasised that the problems of choosing the 'correct' price in the tort action also occur in the other techniques—in choosing, for example, an optimal tax. Thus this difficulty does not allow us to choose tort actions over other methods as a means of coping with externalities.

A more likely criterion, which would lead to a low priority for torts, is the transaction cost of the alternative methods open. It is perfectly feasible to stop household pollution with regulations referring to smokeless fuel but it is a flight of fantasy to imagine a society in which each household sues the households using smokey fuels.

Nevertheless there is in principle scope for further development in the use of tort actions to deal with externalities which would be much hastened by widening the definitions of property and of economic loss and by moving from a fault liability system to some of the features of a strict liability system.

STRICT LIABILITY, COURT AWARDS AND ECONOMIC BEHAVIOUR

A consideration so far hinted at but which ought now to be faced is whether a court award is designed simply to compensate the plaintiff or whether it is also intended to alter the behaviour of the defendant. This is the distinction between prices that lead to a new income distribution and those which also directly produce a new resource use.

The difference can be seen in a fine by Torbay magistrates on Shell Tankers (UK) Ltd of £30,000 when the costs of sea and shore cleaning after an oil spillage were given as £19,400. It is quite possible that the tanker company would be prepared to pay that price to discharge the oil and to go on doing so, just as some car owners regard parking fines as a price to be paid for parking. If such were the case, then there would be an income distribution but no change in economic behaviour.

If we call the sum required to make the defendant change his behaviour D, and the sum necessary to return the plaintiff to his original position P, then we have the following classification:

1   If the court awards P and P is greater than or equal to D then both results are achieved.
2   If the court awards P and P is less than D then the only result is that the plaintiff is compensated.

3   If the court awards D and D is greater than or equal to
    P then both results are achieved.
4   If the court awards D and D is less than P then the
    defendant changes his behaviour but the plaintiff is
    uncompensated.

In some cases, of course, stopping future torts cannot
possibly restore the victim if he has already lost his life
although his dependants might regain their market position. The Niigata Minimata case and the DC10 air crash
are cases in point.[13]

A related classification helps us to choose between
injunctions, fines and leaving the market to operate.[14] The
main criterion used is the minimisation of costs in relation
to benefits.

1   A injunction is issued against X, and thus Y's property
    rights are enforced, if it is cheaper for X to change his
    behaviour. A trifling tresspass might fall into this cate-
    gory.
2   X is made to compulsorily purchase Y's property rights
    if the transaction costs of determining the 'correct'
    resource allocation are very high. A planning decision
    for a large project involving the destruction of many
    houses is likely to fall in this category and expecially so
    if large numbers are involved.
3   X has a right, and is bought off by Y, when this has
    lower transaction costs than any of the alternatives. A
    dispute about a right of way might fall into this cate-
    gory.
4   X's rights are supported by the court at a judicially
    determined price because it is clear that the market will
    produce a 'wrong' resource use and the transaction
    costs of identifying the 'right' price are too high. This
    too is likely in the large-number case. A case involving
    one rich party and many poor parties in which the
    former could 'buy' a sub-optimal resource use that
    might be in his own interest only would fall into this
    category.

This amounts to saying that there are commonsensical ways of proceeding about these matters and they are attractive when the guidelines provided by neoclassical economics make such heavy demands on information that is not easy to come by.

It was emphasised earlier that United Kingdom approaches to economic loss tend to be fault-based. This position is now under pressure with the development of 'strict liability'. Just as the doctrines regarding economic loss seem to be more developed in the United States, so strict liability is further developed in the United States than in the United Kingdom.

Previously, if in all innocence a customer was provided with a defective good then the attitude of the law was that that was a normal risk of life and no individual could be expected to be protected from such risks. The strict liability doctrine is that persons should be protected from such ebbs and flows of life at least in so far as between any two parties any burden should fall on those best able to bear it even though they were not at fault in any normal sense of the word. Effectively this is a redistribution of property rights in that unlucky customers now have a different set of expectations.

Two cases of interest in the law of contract are *H. Kendall & Sons* v. *Wm Lillicoe & Sons Ltd* and *Ashington Piggeries Ltd* v. *Christopher Hill Ltd*.[15] The plaintiff had in the former case bought poultry feed from the defendant and in the latter case the plaintiff had bought herring meal from the defendant. In both cases the foodstuff was found to be defective and there was no method by which its toxic nature could have been identified by the supplier. In both cases the supplier who, it was common ground, had not be negligent, lost the case.

The rationale for these developments has a number of arguments which are really founded in consideration of what the judges deem to be appropriate social policy.

Some would hold that the supplying firms have a moral responsibility in that they have much economic and commercial power and the buyer has very little and that they are thus more able to take the slings and arrows of fortune just as they would any other trade risk.

A different approach is that in mass production there are likely to be relatively and absolutely more errors than in craft production and that the firms should bear the disadvantages of mass production just as they bear the advantages eagerly enough.

A further possibility is that the doctrine of strict liability will lead firms to higher standards of quality control as it will be worth the firm's while to trade off the costs of higher quality control against the risks of strict liability actions.

Further, the costs, in relation to his income and assets, of one individual going to court against a large modern corporation are quite different from the proportionate burden of their costs and so in a world of only fault liability the advantages are all with the strong.

It may be that the development of strict liability will have its major effect on the size of insurance premiums and in the drafting of policies carefully distinguishing between shoddy, defective and unsafe goods. Any such higher premiums can be expected to lead to higher prices for the products so that the customers become the main sources of finance for those of their number who are unfortunate in the particular example that they purchase. If this does become the pattern then the strict liability doctrine is certainly not arming the poor against the rich.

A final point of interest to the economist is that many of these discussions are cast in the form of focusing on the distribution of income between the parties—that is, a discussion of fairness and equity. This tendency should be resisted. Income distributions cannot normally be separated from questions of resource allocation. A change in one implies a change in the other.

In these circumstances, judges cannot correctly persuade themselves that their decisions are of solely legal interest; however tiresome it may be for them, they cannot be economically neutral.

NOTES

1   Supply of Goods (Implied Terms) Act, 1973.

2 K. J. Lancaster, 'A new approach to demand theory', *Journal of Political Economy* vol. XXIV (1966).
3 Information from the *Daily Telegraph*, 4 August 1975.
4 R. Coase, 'The problem of social cost', *Journal of Law and Economics*, vol. IV (1960).
5 *Sturgess* v. *Bridgeman* (1879) 11 Ch. D. 852.
6 R. N. McKean, 'Implications of some changing property rights', *Quarterly Journal of Economics* (1960).
7 P. Stein and J. Shand, *Legal Values in Western Society* (Edinburgh: Edinburgh University Press, 1974).
8 A. Prosser, *Torts* (London: Butterworth, 11th edn, 1975).
9 J. Heydon, *Economic Torts* (London: Butterworth, 1971).
10 *Weller & Co.* v. *National Foot and Mouth Disease Research Institute* (1966) 1QB 569.
11 F. I. Michelman, 'Property, utility and fairness', *Harvard Law Review*, vol. 80 (1967).
12 E. J. Mishan, *Cost-Benefit Analysis* (London: Allen & Unwin, 2nd edn, 1975).
13 A. Morishima, 'Damage functions from the legal perspective Japanese legal experience' in Environmental Damage Costs (Paris: OECD, 1974).
14 C. Calabresi, 'Transaction costs, resource allocation and liability rules', *Journal of Law and Economics*, vol. X (1968).
15 *Ashington Piggeries Ltd* v. *Christopher Hill Ltd* (1971) 1 All ER 847. *Henry Kendall & Sons* v. *William Lillicoe & Sons Ltd and others* (1968) All ER 444.

APPENDIX: THE MARKET PRICE OF HUMAN LIFE

The problem of valuing human life in court compensation awards is common to that of valuing human life in cost-benefit work, in evaluating the economics of health programmes and elsewhere. It will be not surprising that there is not yet any reliable way of placing a money value on human life and the attempts to do so have tended to bring cost-benefit work into disrepute, at least at the journalistic level. It is important to emphasise that to not compensate—that is, to give human life a price of zero—is just as arbitrary and inaccurate a procedure. Any court award is an estimate and is thus vulnerable to criticism and any alternative award is just as open to an alternative set of criticisms. The important points are to make the procedures used in reaching an award explicit and the value system behind them explicit and to be quite clear that at this moment any award is the result of an intuitive process that tries to reflect the society's priorities as they are perceived by a judge.

The first step is to decide the purpose of the award which might be, for instance, to return the plaintiff to his original position in terms of purchasing power in the market. In addition, a further purpose might be to compensate in monetary terms for the various forms of psychological loss such as distress and embarrassment at a permanent injury, pain, or the emotional loss suffered by members of the family of an injured party.

One possible approach to identifying prices to measure one or all of these variables is to adopt a version of the insurance principle. It could be argued that by their attention to insurance persons do in fact indicate the monetary value they put on their own lives. This is not quite the case, for their premiums, if any, show the cover they can buy, which is not the same thing. One possibility is, of course, a comprehensive state insurance policy and the elimination of court cases.

A different approach is not to pay a plaintiff what he would have gained from an insurance policy based on actuarial principles but to pay him the present value of the income that he would otherwise have earned. The emphasis could be on the net or gross change in the national income as a result of the accident.

The present value of the losses suffered by the other members of the family is fraught with difficulties. If the deceased were an elderly dependant then the family might actually be better off in material terms as a result of the death! There is no market in happiness and attempts to price psychological losses should be overtly intuitive.

Chapter 3

Monopolistic Problems and Legal Solutions

INTRODUCTION

The possibility of manoeuvring monopolistic firms into new patterns of behaviour that are seen as more consistent with the public interest than their earlier behaviour has long been a possible economic role for the law. This chapter specifies the problems of monopolised markets as they are seen by economists and the role of law both in general and in this particular context as it is seen by lawyers. It does not offer a comprehensive history of the legislation or a blow by blow account of the cases; there are probably quite enough such accounts already available.[1]

The approaches that we seek to explain and discuss are that in the United States the assumption underlying the legislation is that competitive markets are in the public interest and that monopolised markets are not, while the United Kingdom approach is much more ambivalent and *ad hoc* in its nature. So unambiguous is the United States approach that a merger leading to monopolised markets 'is not saved because on some ultimate reckoning of social, or economic, debits and credits, it may be deemed beneficial'.[2] The United Kingdom attitude is a good deal less aggressive for there is both an administrative and a judicial process, separate from one another, that attempt just such a reckoning.

MONOPOLISED MARKETS AND THEIR ECONOMIC PROBLEMS

Although there is widespread suspicion among laymen of monopolies, the theoretical case against monopoly is really rather weak by the highest standards of intellectual rigour and of statistical testing. The outcome is really rather nearer the Scottish verdict of 'not proven' than either 'innocent' or 'guilty'. Economists have pondered and researched monopolies and their associated restrictive practices a great deal but there is only a single adverse comment against the profit-maximising monopolist that will hold good all the time and everywhere. It is because there is only one such comment that so much has been written for it was important and difficult to attempt to establish the generality of the other critiques on offer.

It is always true that profit-maximising monopolists charge a price that exceeds marginal cost. This means that the money price exaggerates the true cost of production in the form of alternatives forgone. As in the externality case, this leads to a non-optimal set of prices and a consequent misallocation of resources. This holds good, as do all of the following remarks, not only for the idealised form of single-firm monopoly but for any firm which can by altering its output alter the price of its product.

It is often, but not necessarily, true that monopolistic firms produce at an output rate which is not the minimum unit cost rate of output for a given technology and a given set of wage, rent and interest levels.

It is often, but not necessarily, true that monopolies earn super-normal profits which are profit levels greater than those necessary to maintain the firm in business.

It so happens that the opposite holds on all these three points in the perfect competition case when market prices do equal marginal costs, the firm does produce at a rate which minimises unit costs and only normal profits are earned in the long run.

This at least appears to be an hostile case against monopolised markets but the whole critique is rather non-operational for they compare a real market form with an idealised form of the market. The perfect competition model has great power in helping us understand and analyse real world markets but in public policy matters we have to compare one real market form with other real market forms and the role of the law is to generate the form of the market that we prefer out of those actually available. It might seem that we would prefer more competitive markets to less competitive markets but the 'second best theory' allows no such conclusion for it prevents us from scientifically ranking one imperfect market against another. If we do have to choose then a judicial process is one technique open to us, for the conventional welfare theory of the firm is very little help.

So far the emphasis has been on price relative to cost, output relative to the unit cost-minimising output and profits relative to the minimum profits required to sustain the firm in long-run production. The layman's hostility to monopoly tends to emphasise the absolute level of prices and profits. This factual question has not been answered in any manner that would lead to a general conclusion. A wide range of profits and price levels are found in monopoly and it is quite clear that some monopolies do earn low levels of return on their capital and some do go bankrupt. There remains, however, a widespread suspicion that monopoly prices and profits are higher than would be enjoyed by the same firms if they were to face more competition. The fact that this has not really been established by the highest econometric tests does not much hinder the development of public policy, for legislation is based on what is thought to be the case rather than what is the case.

Three other widely held criticisms of monopoly are rather more in the nature of folklore than rigorous analysis. They are that monopolists suppress new innovatory products and techniques, that they engage in 'unfair competition' and that, due to the absence of competition, such firms are less efficient than they would otherwise be. Economists have devoted themselves to these problems[3] and have failed to produce unambiguous results. Like all folklore they are correct some of the time in respect of some of the parties but they do not hold good for all monopolists all of the time.

Given these various criticisms of quite different nature and weight the United States view that competition is the preferable market form seems quite plausible as does a

legislative programme that then unambiguously uses the
law to promote competitive markets.

However, the real world turns out not to be quite so
simple for there are both folkloric and analytic reasons
which may be advanced in favour of monopolised
markets. They probably have more power when the
comparison is between a real world monopoly and some
other real world market.

Among the folkloric arguments are that monopolies
generate research and development programmes and that
they can gain access to scale economies not available when
the same output is produced by a number of smaller firms.
The latter point is typically folkloric in nature and at best is
true of some firms some of the time. The research and
development argument is rather more obscure for we
cannot say that such research and development is 'good'
unless we know both its opportunity costs and the opportunity costs of promoting the same research and development by some other means.

Neither of these points fits particularly well into the
conventional theory of the firm for they deal not with
comparative static comparisons but with economic behaviour in an economy of dynamic change.

The more analytic argument in favour of monopoly also
involves a departure from traditional theory of the firm. In
place of a profit-maximising monopolist, it is possible to
think of a firm—particularly in the case of a large firm—
as a coalition of interest groups. The interest groups
concerned are the management, workers, shareholders and
customers and they have quite different legal status and
unequal bargaining power which itself varies from firm to
firm and time to time.

This means that the outcome of the bargaining between
the parties to the coalition is indeterminate; no single
interest group can expect to achieve all its aims so it settles
for a particular outcome knowing that *to withdraw from
the coalition is to risk a worse outcome*. The position is
further complicated by the presence of sub-groups within
the parties to a coalition; there are conflicting interests
between the workers making one model of a car who are

given a bonus at the expense of workers in another part of the same factory. Another complication is that a given interest group must choose between outcomes that exhibit opposing features—to choose overtime now may be to choose short-time working or unemployment later. The customer who enjoys a low price now may drive the supplying firm bankrupt and suffer no supplies in the future.

It is quite plausible that many interest groups concerned with monopolies in the real world give a higher priority to a known present outcome than to an unknown future outcome which might be better or worse with respect to prices, output and employment. Such attitudes tend to sustain existing monopolies, for one of the attractions that they offer is stability and a quiet life.

Stability may be valued not only by those interest groups who benefit immediately and directly but also by society at large, for the interdependence of modern societies means that stability in one sector helps to generate stability in others: a housewife may enjoy paying low prices at a supermarket but those very low prices threaten to create unemployment possibly including members of her own family.

While one of the benefits of monopoly may be a quiet life, that very approach is an intuitive response to two rather technical questions. The quiet life emphasis is really an assumption that society is not willing to pay the transaction costs of seeking and attaining any preferable alternative outcomes from those available to the coalition. Neither this assumption, nor its opposite, has any real basis save that of intuition. The second technical point centres on whether anything might be said of an *a priori* nature with respect to the equilibrium or optimality properties of the outcome in coalition bargaining. An equilibrium outcome (that is an outcome that precludes any change to a different outcome) is only really likely in 'zero sum two person games' which means two competing parties in a context where the total benefits to be shared between them is constant.[4] This seems to exclude equilibrium outcomes in most bargaining of a monopolistic kind and, indeed, there is a general conclusion in economics that the results of bargaining between social groups will lack the kind of coherence found in individual bargaining.[5]

The 'quiet life' benefits of monopoly, then, are unproved but widely believed in.

A quite different analytic point in favour of monopoly is the case for natural monopolies which argues that the real resource cost for a given output may be less if the output is provided by a single firm than by a number of competing firms. A simple example is that two competing telephone companies need two sets of plant, and to dig up the road twice, in order to provide the same number of phones as would have been managed by one company. Similar arguments apply to many public utilities. This is one of the best-established interconnections between law and economics which often leads to the granting of monopoly licences and franchises and then control of prices by administrative bodies such as the Traffic Commissioners. An alternative is to take the monopoly into public ownership such as the London Transport Executive. This argument for a state role in the economy exercised by legal means was recognised at the height of nineteenth-century *laissez-faire* economics by the common carrier legislation of that era.

This catalogue of advantages and disadvantages helps to legitimise the United Kingdom approach to monopoly legislation which is based on the twin premises that there are questions to be asked and that their answers will differ from case to case, for there is little in the way of general answers of wide applicability. This rather agnostic approach is, of course, reinforced by the 'second best theory' which holds that, in this context, there is no *a priori* reason for believing that the elimination of a single monopoly will *by itself* produce a better resource use.

As it happens, most monopoly problems that have generated public discussion have concerned industrial structure and the level of absolute prices and profits rather than the economist's characteristic concern with relative prices. It also so happens that the effective arguments within

Parliament leading to a particular form of monopoly policy have been of the folkloric kind. Alternatively, the arguments have been overtly political—concerned, for example, with great economic power in the hands of those not directly accountable to Parliament. This latter viewpoint is rather obscure for it has to assume that the legal acts of such monopolies are against the public interest without being illegal. The implication is that such discretion should not be in private hands. Only recently have public corporations begun to be placed under the same legal obligations as private corporations with respect to problems such as defective work. (Section 29 of the Post Office Act conferred immunity on the GPO with respect to negligent work; it was not until *Dutton* v. *Bognor Regis UDC* (1972 QB373) that local authority building inspectors could be held responsible for negligent inspection of building foundations.)

United Kingdom monopoly policy thus has its basis in rather unclear political judgements and in widely held unproved attitudes but it does not run counter to economic analysis apart from the small attention to relative price ratios. The existence of a recognised monopoly problem does not itself imply that the courts and the judicial processes are the appropriate technique to deal with the problem and this latter question of method cannot be answered until we have faced the question of what a law is and what tasks it is perceived as fulfilling.

THE THEORY OF LAW AND ITS APPLICABILITY TO ECONOMIC PROBLEMS[6]

Any system of laws involves a set of rules operated by the individual members of a group in which each person accepts rules that restrain his own freedom of action in return for the same restrictions on others. Some such restrictions are mutually symmetrical: the laws which govern my physical violence to my neighbour also govern his violence to me. Other laws are asymmetrical; the laws which govern a merger between two small shopkeepers differ from those governing a merger between two large firms.

The specification of what constitutes a 'good' law constantly returns to the three ideas of justice, order and freedom. (Some laws, of course, such as traffic regulations, are really administrative methods of seeking to increase utility at minimum cost.) Many laws, and certainly many monopoly laws, specify minimum standards of behaviour rather than demand a particular behaviour which means that by telling a firm what it may not do they leave the firm discretion about what it does do and thus produce indeterminate results.

The ideas of Hobbes with respect to law were rather similar to those of the modern economist with respect to coalitions, for he envisaged a social contract which men made with one another in order to escape a state of nature in which there were no laws. Each man gave up the right to govern himself on condition that every other man did the same and in forgoing some freedom he gained some justice and order. The applicability to the economic behaviour of firms is clear: the interest groups within a firm accept some restraints upon their behaviour and gain the benefits of knowing other firms are also restrained in their behaviour. Such a process is unlikely to produce any particular price and output of the kind familiar from neoclassical economics because it is not clear to all the parties how far they should take this process of accepting restraints for the sake of gaining restraints on others.

Given that there is discretion about how far the law on mutual behaviour between firms should be developed, the distinction arises between law as it is and law as it ought to be. This distinction rather escaped mediaeval considerations of natural law which failed to separate law from morality by focusing on what a good man ought to do; but the Victorian philosopher Austin was at pains to make the distinction between law as it is and as it ought to be. A discussion of law as it ought to be needs an answer to a prior question concerning the form of a good society. A discussion, then, of what is a 'good' monopoly law forces us back to a discussion of what is a 'good' economic society.

The Austinian problem is to consider the kind of society

assumed by the law to be better than the society it seeks to improve. In the United States monopoly law the assumption behind the legislation is that a competitive society is better than a monopolised one; the United Kingdom legislation shares this view but is more ready to recognise some exceptions. We have seen that this view that a more competitive economy is better than a less competitive economy lacks a really rigorous base in analysis for the argument that prefers perfect competition to monopoly is not relevant to the choice that we have to make. A further difficulty is to find an explicit criterion to judge the outcomes of monopoly legislation which is other than a rule-of-thumb.

A point to note at this stage is that the use of judicial procedures in the field of monopoly behaviour leads, like all judicial processes, to an emphasis on precedent, consistency and certainty and these may be preferred to the uncertain tides of fortune in competitive markets. An example is that the insistence on precedent means that the decisions of the courts legitimise subsequent behaviour which might otherwise be open to question.

Adam Smith's system of thought which favoured competition within a market system and the view that if all persons acted in their own best interests then the public interest would also be advanced has permeated the legal ordering of the economy. It was long held, for instance, that there was no real problem with respect to exchange and trade, including the trade of a monopolist, for if a trade was voluntarily entered into then it must be Pareto efficient in that the two parties would not trade if one of the parties was going to be worse off after the exchange. If a trade was voluntarily entered into then it was concluded that no party was worse off.

English contract law still has some of this buccaneering spirit which assumes that each buyer and seller can look after himself. The economist would enter three reservations to the attitude that a freely entered contract must produce a better world than otherwise. First, it is rather ingenuous to describe a purchase from a monopolist such as a water company, selling an essential product with no real substitute, as a freely entered contract. The buyer may choose more or less water according to the price but the freedom to go without water at all has no real operational significance for most people. Secondly, the benefits claimed for the freely entered contract assume an equal distribution of information which is certainly not present in the garage making a car sale to the average motorist. (The law and economics of information are pursued in the next chapter.) Thirdly, parties may be restrained from entering into a mutually advantageous bargain as the outcomes of such bargains may be one of a number of possibilities and if one of the parties were a monopolist then the actual outcome is weighted in his favour with respect to income distribution and resource allocation. Monopoly law thus trades off a conception of justice against freedom to enter a contract.

The law had developed a number of remedies for dealing with 'unfair' outcomes but they relate to special relationships such as parent – child, trustee – beneficiary, and so on, and have little application to the commercial world. In economic relationships the restrictions on continuing acceptance of the results of bargains have centred on the restraint of trade doctrine. This is seldom invoked for the general support of freely entered contracts is still upheld. The restraint of trade doctrine has been applied to employment contracts between a firm and a non-unionised worker (*Eastham* v. *Newcastle United Football Club Ltd* (1964) Ch 223,428). The courts have been much more reluctant when the contract is between two firms; *Texaco Ltd* v *Mulberry Filling Station Ltd* (1972) 1 All ER 513,555) involved a contract between a large oil company and a garage to sell only one brand of petrol; the contract was upheld despite a claim of coercive inequality. The inability of the courts to adapt contractual rules to different contexts has led to the special legislation on exclusion clauses discussed in a later chapter and the development of special bodies like the Monopolies Commission and the Monopolies and Restrictive Practices Court.

The recognition that the restraint of trade doctrine was inappropriate for the protection of the public interest is well founded. *Mogul Steamship Co.* v. *McGregor Gow & Co.* (1892) AC 25 is a tort of conspiracy case involving a restrictive cartel that was putting the plaintiff out of business. The plaintiff lost his case on the grounds that the cartel members 'pursued to the bitter end a war of competition waged in the interests of their own trade'. This argument is counter-intuitive in holding that a cartel is competitive because it competes against non-members.

These attitudes that favour a freely struck bargain contain the paradox that a freedom *of* contract may enable a firm to achieve such a dominant position in the market that others lose their freedom *to* contract. There is thus an awkward balance in limiting an individual's freedom of trade in order to protect the same freedom of trade for others; and there is thus an inherent ambiguity in legal attempts to restrain trade by monopolists which is reinforced by the general unwillingness of the courts to relieve parties of contracts into which they have freely entered. The ambiguity is slightly relieved by specifying a criterion of public interest rather than private interest in United Kingdom monopoly legislation. This doctrine is at the centre both of the monopoly legislation and of the problems attendant on it.

THE UNITED KINGDOM LEGISLATION, THE JUSTICIABILITY OF THE ISSUE AND THE PUBLIC INTEREST

The problems of assessing monopoly legislation and the public interest are interlocked with the justiciability of the issue—that is, the appropriateness of the judicial process to the solution of monopoly problems. The pragmatic approach to monopoly problems rather characteristic of United Kingdom policy has some basis in economics but it is not at all clear that this kind of approach is well suited to the legal processes.

A brief summary of United Kingdom legislation is necessary. It has created two different institutions. One, the Monopolies Commission, is administrative in nature if interrogatory in its investigations, while the other, the

Restrictive Practices Court, is judicial in nature and in its processes and at least appears to be the same as any other part of the High Court.

The Monopolies Commission need concern us no further than to note that it is an investigatory body that examines the behaviour of large firms and particularly proposed mergers between them. The non-specific 'definition' of the 'public interest' in the enabling legislation, coupled with an exhortatory tone based on an unstated notion of a relationship between competition and efficient resource allocation, reappear in different forms in the whole range of monopoly legislation.

All matters which appear in the particular circumstances to be relevant shall be taken into account and, amongst other things, regard shall be had to the need, consistent with the general economic position of the United Kingdom, to achieve:

(a) the production, treatment and distribution by the most efficient and economical means of goods in such types and quantities, in such volume and such prices as will best meet the requirements of the home and overseas trade:

(b) the organisation of industry and trade in such a way that their efficiency is progressively increased . . .

(c) the fullest use and best distribution of men, materials and industrial capacity . . .

(d) the development of technical improvements and the expansion of existing markets and the opening up of new markets.

This is all cast in ringing terms and is difficult to oppose. It would be even more difficult to use these phrases to generate unambiguous criteria for judgemental use. The absence of prices that do measure costs and benefits at all accurately means that there is plenty of room for disagreement on just which types, quantities and prices of goods 'best meet' the needs of society. Once there are no unambiguous and explicit criteria then any processes, let alone judicial processes, run into difficulty.

The Restrictive Practices Court deals not with single firms and mergers but with trading relationships between firms. The Restrictive Trade Practices Act, 1965 is consistent with widespread views about competitive markets in assuming that such markets are preferable to those with agreed restrictions on trade. The Act follows the layman's intuitive ideas and the economist's 'second best theory' in, having made a general stand in favour of competitive markets, then allowing for exceptions which gain approval by qualifying under one or other of a number of 'gateways'.

Section 21 of the Act specifies these gateways and also has a 'tailpiece' that calls on the court to 'balance' the benefits claimed under gateway against any other ill effects that the restrictive agreement may have on the public. Thus the gateways become necessary but not sufficient conditions for a restrictive agreement to merit the court's approval.

The gateways offer the same scope for interpretation as the earlier definition of the public interest. Leaving aside a gateway that allows an agreement that is a necessary adjunct to some other approved agreement, there are six such gateways:

1   that the agreement is necessary for the protection of the public from physical injury;
2   that a specific or substantial benefit results to the public;
3   that the agreement is necessary as a countermeasure to another's restrictions;
4   that the agreement is necessary to protect the parties against large buyers and sellers;
5   that the removal of the agreement would be likely to have a serious and persistent effect on unemployment;
6   that the abolition of the agreement would result in the reduction of the export business.

The last two qualifying clauses require the judges to exercise forecasting skills that regularly escape others and the clauses offer no help on the allowable magnitudes of export or employment effects. Terms such as 'necessary' and 'specific and substantial' are rather elastic.

Such monopoly legislation is clearly Austinian in being based on a concept of a good society—that is, that such a society is found in competitive market trading adjusted for any effects judged to be contrary to the public interest. The problem lies in defining these effects in such a manner that any given case can be clearly put in one category or another. The practice is less consistent with the idea of a good law in that it is easy to foresee judges reaching opposite conclusions when faced with the same evidence. Lawyers prefer laws that will reliably yield the same decision from any judge faced with the same facts.

A problem becomes justiciable when there is some prospect of certainty, consistency and predictability. It has been claimed that the decisions have been sensitive to the particular judges taking the cases.[7] Even if this is not a widely held view it remains true that this legislation is more vulnerable than most legislation on just this point because of the way in which it is cast.

The 'case by case' approach might seem at first glance to be consistent with normal judicial procedure but in practice the case by case method means no more than that the facts of each case are investigated separately. The method also means that the judges have to engage in economic prediction and exercise their value judgements with respect to the conflicting parties in particular and to public policy in general.

In many respects it is the concept of 'public interest' that is most revealing about the economic analysis of monopoly and the suitability of the problem for the judicial process. The very term draws public attention to the weakness of economic theory in providing a thoroughgoing rationale for monopoly policy; it is an imprecise, immeasurable concept to which legislators must turn because economists have failed to provide anything more precise or measurable.

Some examples will make the point. As drafted, the legislation equates the public interest in paragraph 6 (above) with promoting exports but not with curtailing imports so that two agreements which had the same net effect on the balance of payments would be treated unequally. The Act concentrates on the gross contribution to exports and not on any net effect after allowing for any import content in the exports such as the aluminium content in an exported consumer durable.

In *Associated Transformer Manufacturer's Agreement (1961) 2 All ER233* the court held that 'earnings' meant turnover rather than profit and the interpretation chosen can make a great difference to the outcome of a case. There is an almost medieval discussion in a balancing tailpiece judgement in *Permanent Magnet Manufacturers' Association Agreement (1962) All ER775* of a 'reasonable' price. The obvious comment 'reasonable for whom?' specifies the quandary. Further difficulties follow when a practice produces gains for some and losses to others in the same industry or elsewhere. 'The section, or the Act as a whole, does not in any way indicate how the different interests are to be ranged in order of priority, urgency or weight'.[8] These examples of the manner in which the public interest criterion raises as many problems as it solves may be easily multiplied.

It is not, of course, novel for judges to have to interpret legislation but what is novel is the scope for interpretation. The judges not only have to choose between different accounts of the 'facts' as in a contested crime but also what is and is not an economic 'crime.' In conventional judicial decisions there is little dispute regarding what is or is not a murder, a theft or a restricted parking area, but the Restrictive Practices Court has to decide not only the fact but also, in some sense, what is and is not against the law. The exercise of so much judgement runs counter to Bacon's idea that 'the best law leaves least to the judge's discretion.'

Monopoly legislation is anomalous set against the traditions of English law which has an emphasis on, almost an obsession with, certainty and which requires the judges not to reflect on the good society but to implement the laws which a society does have quite independently of their own views.

It is difficult to resist the view that the 'public interest' is a remarkably unhelpful criterion. This is at least partly because the social interest is not coherent and making markets more competitive is in the interests of some and against the interests of others—that is, it is *ambiguous because the new resource pattern is not Pareto efficient.* Once it is Pareto inefficient then the judges must make value judgements on behalf of society because economists have failed to produce operational criteria for the problem and Parliament has failed to make any such judgements. It is thus also difficult to resist the conclusion that monopoly problems are not really a justiciable issue.

It has to be said that between 1956 and 1965 these difficult judgements were exercised by the government of the day in response to the investigations of the Monopolies Commission. Neither politicians nor businessmen seem to have relished this state of affairs but transferring the decisions to the courts simply created benefits for politicians and burdens for lawyers and leant arbitrary decisions a spurious respectability.

NOTES

1   A. Hunter, *Competition and the Law* (London: Allen & Unwin, 1966).
    A. Hunter, *Monopoly and Competition* (Harmondsworth: Penguin, 1966).
    C. K. Rowley, *The British Monopolies Commission* (London: Allen & Unwin, 1966).
    C. Brock, *The Control of Restrictive Practices* (McGraw-Hill, 1966).
    R. B. Stevens and B. S. Yamey, *The Restrictive Practices Court* (London: Weidenfeld & Nic olson, 1965).
2   *US* v. *Philadelphia National Bank*, 347, US321,371.
3   C. Freeman, *The Economics of Industrial Innovation* (Harmondsworth: Penguin, 1974).
4   E. Roy Weintraub, *Conflict and Co-operation in Economics* (London: Macmillan, 1975).
5   K. Arrow, *Social Choice and Individual Values* (Yale, Mich.: Yale University Press, 1951).
6   P. Stein and J. Shand, *Legal Values in Western Society* (Edinburgh: Edinburgh University Press, 1974).
7   R. B. Stevens and B. S. Yamey, *The Restrictive Practices Court* (London: Weidenfeld & Nicolson, 1965), ch. 1.
8   ibid., p. 87.

Chapter 4

The Law and Economics of Information

This chapter discusses briefly the role of information in the economic process and the reasons for believing that information fails to perform its economic functions at all fully. One way of dealing with the problem—which is that of constructing incentives to invent and innovate—is the use of the law in the form of enforceable property rights in patents and copyrights.

It is widely recognised that information and technological advance is central to the problems of economic growth, related conservation problems and many other contemporary problems, but the role of information is rather less emphasised in neoclassical economics at the introductory level although it is central to the whole notion of advantageous trading.

Nevertheless, both economists and lawyers have persisted in a rather ambivalent attitude to those who trade information or who trade because they have different information from the other party. Difficulties, both moral and economic, commence when the parties possess very unequal information as in cases where farmers sell land to an oil company when the former are unaware of its oil-bearing characteristics which are known only too well to the oil company. Another example occurs when antique dealers buy from innocent members of the public unaware of the true nature of their possession. In such cases only the buyer will feel that he has unambiguously traded to a better position, for the seller, *even though he voluntarily entered into the bargain*, will come to wish that he had traded on better terms. We need to separate the fact that he was better off in that he did value the money more than the land or *objet d'art* from his subsequent resentment that he would have traded differently if only his information had been different at the time.

The public attitude in these cases of an asymmetric distribution of information is often that something 'unfair' has happened although it is difficult to see much difference in principle from the gains made by an inventor who patents his information. In all cases the information that led to the geological knowledge, the artistic expertise or the invention had to be acquired.

A further example of the ambivalence that is common in both layman's and economist's attitudes to trading in information is the case of 'insider' trading in stocks and shares. A person who possesses knowledge relating to a company before the general public does, because he works for that company, is not expected to deal in those shares and the Stock Exchange or the courts may well take action against him if he does. Yet other cases in which a person trades because he has prior knowledge, such as an oil company buying up land, often anonymously through subsidiary companies, are considered perfectly legal, and often admired, and unequal information is common to most trading.

These points will be taken up later but it is useful to emphasise just how central to the economy is the production, diffusion, storage and use of knowledge.

Some firms trade simply in information and little else and their customers know that alternative methods of attaining the information are likely to be more costly. However resentful he may be of the house agent's fees, the house seller incurs them rather than face the search costs of finding a willing buyer by some other means. Agents— whether they are house, literary or export agents— construct 'markets' in which parties can trade and the commissions paid comes from the economic gains that both buyers and sellers could not otherwise make.

Art and antique dealers are in a rather different category for as well as creating a market they normally hold stocks and trade on their own account in that market and so they not only trade in information but trade advantageously because they have different information in the form of their professional expertise.

Trade unions and professional associations such as the Law Society are only too well aware of the value of information in the form of their members' skill and expertise; they can raise their members' incomes by restricting certain work to them such as property conveyancing in the United Kingdom. It is also in their members' interests to restrict apprentice entry, as did the mediaeval guilds, or in modern times to restrict examination pass-rates in professional examinations. Indeed, the clients of solicitors, doctors and dentists are using professional qualifications as a low search cost method of identifying those who have reliable knowledge.

A last example of the role of information in trading exchanges is the custom of a payment for 'goodwill' in purchasing an established business as customers do use reputations—manifest, for instance, in brand names—as a cheap but imperfect way of identifying reliable sources of supply.

Some of the jargon popularised by Williamson[1] is helpful in structuring an approach to information and markets. He offers, in a related context, three concepts: first, 'bounded rationality', the mental limits which prevent one party perceiving all the implications and potentialities of a situation; 'asset stripping', the practice of buying a company and re-selling it in parts because the buyer realises that this will generate more revenue than the firm is worth as a whole; secondly, 'opportunism', taking advantage of the incomplete information of other parties (the very choice of term implies a hostile moral judgement; and thirdly, 'information impactedness', which means that the true circumstances are known only to some parties and cannot be costlessly discovered by others—circumstances that lead clients to pay commissions to agents rather than face the higher costs of gaining information.

Not only does information have a rather widespread role in economics so that it is a feature of most trading exchanges; it also has rather specific characteristics of its own.

PUBLIC GOODS, STOCKS AND FLOWS

Many of the characteristics of the economics of information

flow from the public goods aspects of information and also the relationship between optimal stocks and flows both from the viewpoint of the public and from that of the private party.

Reference was made in an earlier chapter to the characteristics of a public good. The consumption by one person of a private good excludes another from enjoying that consumption—the man who eats an apple must deny his neighbour the chance of eating that same apple. A man who uses a public good does not exclude his neighbour from that same use; the motorist who sees a traffic light does not stop any other motorist from doing the same.

Much time has been spent by economists trying to identify the 'pure' public good but little time is needed to find products which have the characteristics of a public good and information is a case in point.

The use by one person of information does not stop any other person using the same information and in that sense the stock of information is a public good. The practice of patents and copyrights involves changing a price for the use of information and the pricing of public goods is inconsistent with their nature. The public good aspect of information raises two problems. In the absence of property rights in the information the market system will not produce the optimal output of information as there is little (economic) point in incurring the costs of producing what others may then use free. If the community wishes to encourage the production of information then some sort of patent and copyright system is the obvious strategy for that will establish property rights. However, while this achieves one end it hinders another, for we are not only concerned with the stock of information but its use and, once there is a fee for use of the patented or copyrighted material, then there is likely to be under-use, for the optimal price for a public good is zero. This cleft stick will be taken up later.

Not only are there problems of the optimal stock of information and its optimal use, but if the actual stock of information is not the same as the required stock then there is a problem of the optimal flow of new information which will adjust the actual stock to the optimal stock. The main economic and legal point here is the treatment of research and development.

Bearing in mind the distinction between private and social interests, we will use this structure to examine United Kingdom policy and practice and proposed reforms.

POLICY AND PROBLEMS

Separating the problems of patents from those of research and development is, of course, rather a false distinction but of some pedagogic value and in practice policy changes are sometimes made in one, on the assumption that public policy in the other is remaining constant.

While the patent system has often been criticised for the monopoly power that it confers on the patentee, it has, in different forms, shown great powers of survival. There was a patent system in Venice in 1474 and the United Kingdom Statute Monopoly of 1624 established the practice in Britain. The enduring rationale of the deliberate creation of monopolies has been that the promise of monopoly prices to private parties has attracted a greater volume of resources to inventive activity that is held to be in the public interest. A further supportive point is that it seems fair to the inventor.

There are three ideas implicit in this approach that highlight both its strong and weak points. The notion that changes in money prices will lead to changes in economic behaviour is central to neoclassical economics but it supposes that the persons concerned maximise their economic welfare with reference to material benefits. This is inappropriate as an explanation of the behaviour of the artist or the sole inventor with a good idea. It is difficult to imagine that Shakespeare would have written more or less, or better or worse, if he had had access to an effective copyright law. The manipulation of prices through the patent system as an incentive to inventive behaviour is rather more appropriate to large firms and their research and development efforts than to individual effort.

A second idea in the approach is that more inventive

behaviour is unambiguously good. As we have seen there is some foundation for the idea that a market system leads to underinvestment in inventive activity but unfortunately the analysis is quite unhelpful on just how much more such activity is needed. It is not true that extra innovation is always worthwhile for there is always an alternative opportunity forgone.

A third idea is that of equi-marginal returns. A serious criticism[2] of the patent system is that it encourages the allocation of resources away from non-patentable products to patentable ones. There is nothing to raise the presumption that from the social viewpoint the latter are preferable to the former. The same critic suggests that the copyright laws lead novelists to produce less novels than otherwise to reach a given income. While this is true, it is just as possible that the abolition of copyright laws would lead novelists and artists to take up a different career rather than work harder. We may be fairly sure that wherever the wellsprings of genius may be in cases comparable to those of Michaelangelo or Shakespeare they do not flow from the copyright laws.

The more formal problems of patent and copyright laws lie elsewhere. We need at least some general idea of how much resources we wish to invest in research and development and related activities and some knowledge of just how much we need to change the prices to gain this response—that is, we need to know the supply elasticities. A further rather precise question to which we must return is whether it might be possible to reward inventive and innovative activities without generating monopoly power by the award of a patent.

UNITED KINGDOM PRACTICE

In the United Kingdom, a person granted a patent acquires a right enforceable at law to control the use of his patented discovery for sixteen years subject to the payment of fees to the Patent Office. (In some circumstances the patent may be extended.) The Patent Office is headed by a Comptroller about whose decisions, and those of his patent examiners, appeals may be made to a patent appeals tribunal. Patent actions are heard by High Court judges.

There are four main conditions for a valid United Kingdom patent.[3]

The invention must be fully specified and the patentee identified. The specification must be such than an expert in the field would be able to implement it. The patentee must also specify the scope of the monopoly that he seeks. It is in his interest to make as broad a claim as possible but the broader the claim, the more likely he is to face a challenge, so he must trade off scope against credibility. The inventor is regarded as the first claimant in this country although the Paris (Industrial Property) Convention, to which the major patenting nations subscribe, allows a period of twelve months after filing in any member country to establish a prior claim.

Secondly, the invention must be a 'manner of manufacture'. This term is interpreted rather broadly. Processes may be patented if they lead to a product, while uses may be patented provided they are uses in manufacture and not in consumption. New foods and drugs may be patented only as new chemical products. The main problems centre on new designs such as a chair which are presumably as much to the public benefit as new products but the former are difficult to patent. A main effect is probably to drive firms to emphasise trade names as a means of monopolising sales of a particular design. *R.* v. *PAT ex. parte Swift & Co.* (1962) RPC 37 established that certain types of animal treatments may be patented. Mathematical models, computer programs, and so forth, are not currently patentable. The effective reason in this case seems to be the transaction cost in terms of computer expertise that would need to be transferred to the Patents Office in such an eventuality.

Thirdly, the invention must be novel in the sense of not currently in the public domain.

Fourthly, it must be something which would not be easily anticipated.

These four conditions are only really used if a patent is challenged. Routine cases do not always meet all these conditions because of the resource costs of fully monitoring the applications.

This is a sensible policy which refused to allocate highly valued resources at the margin for the probability of a low return. An awareness of transaction costs is also shown in that hearings in the event of opposition are dealt with quickly by the Patent Office compared with a court case so most firms prefer them. Over 40,000 patents are granted annually and usually less than 100 are contested and less than 50 successfully so.

These figures are explained by the fact that most contested patents are contested by means of infringements and an out-of-court settlement where the claimant 'trades' to a position preferable to observing the patent and the patentee 'trades' to a position better than facing a court action of uncertain outcome. Infringements are also a means of manoeuvring the patentee into granting a licence.

Production licences may be granted by the patentee at his own discretion. The Patents Act, 1949, forces the patentee to grant licences to applicants where the patent relates to food or medicine. The patentee's monopoly powers are also limited by the possibility of a court action on the validity of his patents, the need to pay royalties to any earlier patentee upon whose invention he himself depends, the requirements that he must work the invention which thus stops patents being used to block competitive developments by other firms and by the fact that the Patent Comptroller can be asked to ensure that licences are granted to others on reasonable terms. These provisions serve to limit the monopoly power generated by a patent and, in return, a patent monopoly cannot as such be referred to the Monopolies Commission. Government departments may use a patented invention 'for the services of the Crown' and fix terms later. This provision has been much used by the DHSS.

The problems of the patent system are essentially those of monopoly power—that is, they are problems of prices, incomes and resource allocation and a widespread unease regarding the firms' competitive liveliness. These considerations are cast in the form of comparative static analysis and against a hypothetical criterion at its most powerful when comparing different uses of the same resources. The claimed advantages are cast in a quite different intellectual framework which really centres on different quantities of resources rather than the use of given resources—for these purposes, information, technical expertise and inventions are regarded as a resource.

The kind of questions that are asked with respect to patents are the changes that they produce in the rate and direction of technical innovation, the effect on prices and the diffusion of technical knowledge.

Given the long history of patents and the ferocity with which patentees and the Patent Bar have fought off any suggestion of change, a thorough study of these issues reached surprisingly muted results.[4] With the exception of pharmaceuticals and certain engineering products it was difficult to see that the patent system produced different results from those of a general licensing system. A comparison with a no-patent system concluded that there would be a significant switch of resources away from patentable activities in exactly the manner predicted by neoclassical economics. No doubt when firms had invested in research and development they would simply find some other way of gaining an effective monopoly of its use; such methods might be mergers between forms of restrictive practices. It might well be the one-idea small inventor who would be most disadvantaged by the abolition of the patent system.

It should be noted that one strategy used in some societies such as the USSR is to separate the reward for invention from the rewards from its use. The government rewards innovation with adjudicated awards and the factory making the product pays nothing to the inventor responsible. This distinguishes property rights in the invention from property rights in its use. Such a system does not seem to square with the property rights system in a conventional market economy.

As we have seen, the role of law within the economics of information is to generate a different set of prices—and thus of economic behaviour—from those that would otherwise exist. In practice, most societies find the patent system ineffective for their requirements and construct a system of direct government action through research councils and direct subsidies to universities and research bodies of one kind and another. Where really big risks are involved the patent system may be insufficient inducement and resort may be made to government contracts as in the defence and aerospace industries.

Although most patented products do not enjoy very different profit rates from the norm, some, particularly in ethical drugs, really earn high rates and it may be the hope (as opposed to the probability) that maintains the interests of firms in the patent system. But the following conclusion seems more than plausible: ' . . . the patent monopoly is small beer . . . the patent system is essentially weak and vulnerable . . . but it is an important protection for the small man and the small firm. On balance it is a valuable institution, but its economic value overall is quite modest and it is desirable that extravagant claims should not be made on its behalf.'[5]

NOTES

1 O. Williamson, *Markets and Hierarchies* (London: Collier Macmillan, 1975).
2 A. Plant, 'The economic theory concerning patents for inventions', *Economica*, n.s, vol. III (1935).
3 T. A. Blanco-White, *Patents for Inventions* (London: Stevens, 1973).
4 C. T. Taylor and Z. A. Silbertson, *The Economic Impact of the Patent System* (Cambridge: Cambridge University Press, 1973).
5 ibid., p. 365.

Chapter 5

The Law and Economics of Consumer Protection

'CAVEAT EMPTOR' AND FREEDOM OF CONTRACT

Consumer protection legislation has been one of the growth industries of the twentieth century. We can illumine both the timing and form of this development by setting what is essentially a political response in a context of legal and political ideas. It is a political phenomenon because it is the outcome of a conflict between manufacturers and retailers on the one hand and consumers on the other but it is only conceived as a conflict at all within a particular way of looking at the world.

It is convenient to subsume consumer protection as a part of the law against monopoly with rather similar legal and economic problems to those already noted in the monopoly chapter. The particular characteristics of consumer legislation are that the form of the monopoly problem is manifested in the twin forms of unequal knowledge between the parties and unequal bargaining power between the parties so that some of the concepts are similar to those used in the analysis of patents.

A preliminary point is whether the action should lie against the retailer or the manufacturer or both. Needless to say, practice varies according to the legal nature of the case; the plaintiff chooses to proceed with his case in the form, from those options open to him, which offers him a size of an award and a probability of gaining it that he regards as the most advantageous. Generally, most cases *are* between the consumer and the retailer for the simple reason that the contract is with the retailer which is a clear example of the form of the law helping to determine the economic outcome. Cases may arise in which this is all manifestly 'unfair' to the retailer who was not responsible for the manufacture or design of the good. Few retailers could willingly face such a trading environment so that where the legal relationship is between the retailer and the consumer then the retailer protects himself by insurance or by taking a separate legal action against the manufacturer. The manufacturer may, in his turn, seek to minimise difficulties for his retailers by readily replacing goods, and so forth.

Although the general relationship is between the consumer and the retailer there are exceptions. The consumer may have a good claim against the manufacturer in instances such as direct selling, advertising claims or guarantees. In such cases, the lawyer is often concerned with whether there is, in some sense, a 'contract' and we have already seen in the context of monopoly legislation that the law is reluctant to protect persons from the consequences of contracts into which they have entered. This way of thinking reappears in the field of consumer legislation. A circumstance in which actions may proceed between consumer and manufacturer is that of negligence giving rise to a tort action where the plaintiff must show that the defendant had a duty to take care, that he did not do so and that the breach of duty resulted in foreseeable damage.

However, the problem of whom to sue is a rather technical one and we are more concerned with the rise and form of consumer protection. *Donoghue* v. *Stevenson* (1932) AC 962 concerned a successful action against a ginger beer manufacturer a bottle of whose product contained a partly decomposed snail. Previously, the attitude had been widespread that if manufacturers could be sued 'then it is difficult to see how, if that were the law, trade could be carried on'. This is the floodgates of legislation argument and its weight depends on the size of transaction costs and the scope for insurance. The same problem arises in the introduction of strict liability doctrines. The Donoghue and Stevenson case is therefore a turning point in bringing to the fore a different attitude that was, in the words of Lord Atkins' judgement, 'The rule that you are to love your neighbour becomes in law, you must not injure your neighbour . . . who, then, is my neighbour? The answer seems to be—persons who are so closely and directly affected by my act that I ought reasonably to have them in contemplation.'[1]

The biblical phraseology is not without significance for all law arises and operates within a social context and theological precedents are commanding within a theistic society. While pleasantly free from jargon, Lord Atkins is here hovering on an idea characteristic of modern demand theory as mentioned in an earlier chapter which is that a consumer does not buy a good, he buys the characteristics of a good. The characteristics of ginger beer are partly positive such as its flavour and its aerated nature and partly negative and among the things it is not supposed to contain is a partly decomposed snail.

Any discussion of the problems of consumer protection has as motifs both the conflict between the emphasis on treating people as responsible for the consequences of contracts into which they have entered and leaving them as the occasional victims of their own contracts and also an emphasis on consumer protection by defining the 'contract' so that the parties have a duty to take reasonable care.

RATIONALE FOR CONSUMER PROTECTION

Some sense can be made of consumer protection legislation by using some of the ideas with which we are already familiar—the concepts of trading to the mutual advantage of both buyer and seller, the concept that any such Pareto-efficient trade has an income distribution consistent with it, the concept that the buyer purchases the 'characteristics' of the good including features such as reliability and safety and lastly the concept that the set of prices generated by a *laissez-faire* market economy were widely thought to produce the best allocation of resources.

Until well into the twentieth century, there was very little in the way of consumer protection by the law and the established attitude was summed up in the phrase *caveat emptor*—let the buyer beware. There were, of course, circumstances in which a dissatisfied buyer might turn to the courts for protection—for example, in instances of fraud—and from mediaeval times there were provisions that held innkeepers responsible to their customers for thefts on the premises even when the innkeeper had taken every reasonable precaution. These examples merely show what often holds good in social science problems—that there are very few rules that hold good all the time and everywhere.

The general principle that the buyer should and could look after himself had its roots in the idea that a system of robust trading was a good system in which the final outcome with respect to resource allocation and income distribution was desirable. This attitude was itself supported by three ideas. The value judgment was widespread that if a fool and his money were soon parted then that was no more than was to be expected and was 'right': just as a tone-deaf person could not expect a career as a professional musician, so a fool could not expect to engage in other than foolhardy actions. The second idea which consolidated the *caveat emptor* approach was the Adam Smith argument that a free market led to the best resource use. The third idea, running parallel to the second, was that if a buyer and seller made a 'contract' then, save for such cases as overt fraud, that contract was sacred.

If contracts, voluntarily entered into, were not going to be supported by the courts, then it was believed that fewer people would trade and so there would be less benefit from specialisation and division of labour. This whole system of ideas seemed to be an interlocking whole—and what is more a sensible way of running society, for it was also consistent with the notion of individual freedom and individual responsibility.

This system of values thus gave a low priority to consumer protection. The rising role of consumer protection law is an example of the point that—whatever lawyers claim—the law is not an immutable system but manmade. Changes in the law are largely the result of men perceiving the world differently from hitherto.

At least four reasons may be found for the rise of

consumer protection law and the associated consumer lobbies. First, *caveat emptor* makes much sense in a primitive society where there is little trade but much self-reliance within the family and the village and what trade there is concerns goods such as farm produce where both buyer and seller might be equally knowledgeable. The buyer at the occasional fair or market would indeed be expected to take care, since he might never see the itinerant seller again. In many cases, the value of the sale would in any event be less than the likely transaction costs of going to court.

The twentieth-century consumer lives in a very different world. A far greater proportion of the family consumption of goods and services is bought and the average consumer is at some disadvantage compared to the retailer and manufacturer of electrical goods, consumer durables, and so forth—*that is, information is asymmetrically distributed*. This means that the concept of a bargain struck between equals is quite inappropriate and so, as in the case of monopoly legislation, attempts are made to defend the weaker party against any unfortunate outcomes of the bargains into which he freely enters—because he may have entered them innocently. It should be said that in many trivial transactions the costs of going to court far outweigh the losses and so many breaches of the letter or the spirit of the law go unpunished. The disgruntled shopper simply takes his business elsewhere in future.

If one reason for the attack on *caveat emptor* is because the world is more complex, and the distribution of information and bargaining power unequal, a second reason is that free market systems have come to be seen, at least technically, as not necessarily leading to the optimal use of resources. A third reason is that the value judgement implicit in the 'devil take the hindmost' attitude to the parting of a fool from his money is now much less widely held. People are commonly seen as the products of their own history and environment rather than as responsible in any direct sense for their own foolhardiness.

These changes of emphasis in the way in which the world is perceived have led in the United Kingdom, the United

States and elsewhere to the growth of consumer protection. In the United Kingdom, there has been the Moloney Report, 1962, the Hire Purchase Act, 1964, the Trade Descriptions Act, 1968, the Consumer Council, 1963–71, the Supply of Goods (Implied Terms) Act, 1973, the Unsolicited Goods and Services Act, 1971, the Unfair Contract Terms Act, 1977, a great number of Orders in Council and by-laws following Weights and Measures Acts and also legislation relating to particular industries such as the Hotel Proprietors Act, 1956, or to particular practices such as the Trading Stamps Act, 1964.

Having indicated the burgeoning nature of consumer protection, we do not seek a detailed account of the legislation as it now stands but a discussion of the main legal and economic concepts and problems.

CONSEQUENCES AND COSTS
OF CONSUMER PROTECTION

The general form of the economics of consumer protection involves two issues. The legislation produces a different outcome with respect to resource allocation, prices and income distribution to that which would otherwise occur. The redistribution is from the weaker to the stronger with respect to bargaining power and expertise and is an attempt to assuage the effects of the unequal initial distribution of information and economic power. The second economic theme running through consumer protection is that it is not free: if companies are put in positions where they become more open to court actions for negligence, shoddy goods, and so forth, then they will devote more resources to quality control or even withdraw from some markets. These actions lead both to higher market prices and to resource effects elsewhere in other sectors of the economy.

Technically, following the equi-marginal rule, companies would be advised to allocate extra resources to quality control while the marginal cost of those resources is less than the marginal cost of the legal actions thus avoided.

One of the chief features of the legal development of consumer protection was the changed role of the freedom of contract which, as we have seen, was viewed as one of the foundations of a well-organised society.

A manoeuvre taken up by manufacturers and retailers was for the 'contract' to state expressly that the seller was not to be held liable. An example of such an exemption clause would be a cloakroom ticket stating: 'The Company does not accept responsibility for goods deposited with it.' Examples of such exemption clauses were and still are found on tickets, and posted on walls in shops, garages and car parks. In such cases it is difficult to believe in practice that there is an express agreement between both parties in any normal sense of the term. In many cases, such as the Terms and Conditions of a railway company's ticket (*Thompson* v. *London, Midland & Scottish Railway Co.* (1930) 1 KB 41) or those of a commercial car park (*Thornton* v. *Shoe Lane Parking Ltd* (1970) 1 All ER 686) it is both unreal and unreasonable to think that customers can or do read such conditions. (The fact that they would be well advised to do so or that they should do would be the attitude under the earlier *laissez-faire* attitude.) To talk of an 'agreement' or a 'contract' in such circumstances is to do violence to the language.

One aspect of the development of consumer protection, then, has been the narrower and narrower interpretation of exemption clauses by the courts and indeed an increasing reluctance to pay any attention to them at all if there is any hint of unequal bargaining power or information or if they represent an attempt to make the buyer sign away his common law rights. (At one stage in the United Kingdom, motor-car manufacturers were giving guarantees as part of the conditions of sale which, had they been accepted by the courts would have given the buyers fewer rights than they would have had under common law if they had not received any guarantees.)

A second feature of the attack on freedom of contract was the doctrine of 'fundamental breach of contract.' This doctrine involves eliminating the details of any contract to isolate the fundamental nature of the agreement. The doctrine may be exemplified by *Karsales (Harrow) Ltd* v. *Wallis* (1956) 1 WLR 956. The purchaser of a car was supported by the court in rejecting a vehicle which he wanted to purchase through hire-purchase in the form of the car being sold to the finance company and then hired to him. He rejected the car on the grounds that it was fundamentally different, when delivered to him, from the state it was in when inspected and the agreement made. It had to be towed to his house, valves were burned out, two pistons were broken and new tyres had been replaced by old. This is a rather extreme case of fundamental breach of contract since, as Lord Birkett said in judgement, 'a car that will not go is no car at all'. The fundamental breach of contract technique has been a useful way of protecting buyers, although there is a difficult area requiring discretion and judgement where the complaint is not that the good is quite different from that ordered but that it is of poor or shoddy quality.

Discretion and judgement are the order of the day; some breaches are more fundamental than others and there is room for legitimate differences of opinion. The problem centres, so to speak, on why the car does not go. An unconnected electrical lead is hardly a fundamental breach of contract. Sometimes, of course, the sum effect of a number of small defects amounts to a fundamental breach of contract. *Yeoman Credit Ltd* v. *Apps* (1962) 2 AB 508 concerned a car that did in fact go but it took one-and-a-half hours to travel three miles. It so happens that the examples quoted are all concerned with hire-purchase but it should be emphasised that the doctrine of fundamental breach of contract is of general applicability. It has been used to protect consumers in 'contracts' dealing with storage, cleaning and transport of goods.

The third form of attack on exemption clauses within freedom of contract has been to focus on who *agreed* to the contract. On occasions, this has enabled action to be taken against a company's servants rather than the company or against a company's sub-contractors.

This area of the law has been a battleground of redrafted exemption clauses intended to circumvent a court decision, a further decision and then a further cycle. There is indeed a fundamental conflict between enforcing freely entered contracts and consumer protection. Both seem quite worthy aims. In general the attitude of the courts is still that contracts must be enforced and relatively little attention is paid to the fact that some contracts are not freely negotiated in any normal sense save where the courts are required to do so by law. The problem has been neatly summarised by Lord Devlin: 'The Courts could not relieve in cases of hardship and oppression because the basic principle of freedom of contract included freedom to oppress.'

Freedom of contract between equals is a myth because if the two parties were equal in every relevant respect then the outcome would be certain and there would be nothing to negotiate. Nevertheless, freedom of contract, and if necessary between unequals, was and still is highly valued. In 1875, the then Master of the Rolls said: 'If there is one thing more than another public policy required it is that men of full age and competent understanding shall have the utmost liberty of contracting, and that their contracts when entered into voluntarily shall be held sacred and shall be enforced by Courts of Justice.'[2] While fewer persons would now give the weight of 'If there is one thing which more than another public policy required . . . ', there is still widespread agreement that freedom and sanctity of contract are necessary pre-conditions for Pareto-efficient solutions in a market economy. The consumer lobby's point is one we have met before—the fact that the two parties traded does indeed mean that trade is better than non-trade for both buyer and seller and in that sense the contract is Pareto efficient, but there are many Pareto-efficient outcomes and the actual outcome in a world of unequal bargaining power and information may well be one that many people would regard as 'unfair' with respect to both income distribution and resource allocation.

Lawyers—and social scientists in general—have been sympathetic to this point though doubtless it has been expressed in different jargon. However, the legal history of the problem has tended to obscure the essential point at issue. Lawyers' energies have been taken up with the problem of attaining the new outcome by debating questions such as actions against the servants of the company instead of the company and whether the seller could be liable for negligence as well as fraud for somebody other than the purchaser—as in *George* v. *Skivington* 1869 LR v Exc 1 which concerned a man who bought a negligently made-up hairwash compound for his wife from a chemist.

In the development of the common law, by means of legal decisions, it seems understandable that attention has centred not on the desirability or otherwise of the outcome but on the technical problems of attaining that outcome. Change was slow because the system of social and legal ideas in tandem with a market economy were all in favour of free markets and 'devil take the hindmost' and therefore all the precedents were in favour of not protecting the customer from his own mistakes any more than the seller.

Similarly, the legislation was focused on the technical problems of bringing the buyer and seller to the market with a more equal distribution of bagaining power and information and also of defining the 'market' as the purchase and sale of a 'good' in which the 'good' was regarded not only as the physical object but also as the sum of its characteristics such as quality, reliability and the nature of any guarantee and the opportunities to return the good to the seller for the original price and thus re-contract to the original pre-sale position.

The Consumer Protection Act, 1961, expressly provides for civil liability for the purchaser against the seller if the seller fails to comply with his duties under the Act. Section 3(1) states: ' . . . a duty . . . is owed to him by any other person who may be affected by the contravention . . . and a breach of that duty is actionable.' At one time, it was possible for both criminal and civil actions to be proceeding at the same time and out of phase with one another and with much duplication of effort and evidence. The Criminal Justice Act, 1972, has minimised this problem. The Consumer Protection Act gives the Home Secretary a general power to make regulations to protect the public from the hazards of death, injury and disease.

The Trading Stamps Act, 1964, dealt with the problem that in many trading stamp schemes the holder of the books of stamps exchanged the books for the goods without any money changing hands. If the goods turned out to be unsatisfactory, the Sale of Goods Act, 1893, would not apply as no money was involved. The Trading Stamps Act dealt with this problem and put the stamp collector in a position to demand cash instead of goods. Some members of the consumer protection lobby[3] feel that the Act did not go far enough in that it failed to provide that insolvent trading stamp promoters should have sufficient finance to redeem all stamps already issued. It is unclear why the creditors' hierarchy in the event of a bankruptcy should be changed in this way, and why the customers of an insolvent trading stamp company differ from the customers of an insolvent shop is obscure.

The Hire Purchase Act, 1965, was a reform and codification Act relating mainly to the circumstances in which the finance company could repossess the goods and on what terms. It was generally premised on the view that the buyer needed protection. One of its most interesting features was the 'cooling-off period' which allowed agreements signed in the home to be revoked by the buyer within three clear days. This provision is unique in the law of contract and is designed to protect those vulnerable to high-pressure doorstep salesmanship. Expressed in economic jargon, it holds that the *tatonnement* process may yield a non-Pareto result if one party has been misled or bamboozled with poor information by the other. It is symptomatic of the whole consumer protection lobby that the seller cannot contract out within three days and the value judgements underlying the current legislation may be focused by quoting the opposite value judgements: ' . . . the question is whether the scales have been tilted too heavily against the tader. The wider use and experience of consumer credit since pre-war days should be expected to reduce the need for special protection . . . the individual should accept the responsibility of deciding whether to make use of this form of credit. Having entered into the agreement, he ought to be held to the instalments and in the event of default should be prepared to face the consequences.'[4]

The Advertisements (Hire-Purchase) Act, 1967, provides that all advertisements should state clearly the initial deposit, the number and frequency of payments and the total purchase price and the cash price. If the interest rate is quoted, then it must be the 'true' interest rate calculated by a particular formula. The effect of this provision seems to have been that the interest is rarely mentioned in advertisements at all. An Act which forced the statement of the 'true' interest rate would have been very useful to the buyer.

The Misrepresentation Act, 1967, made it possible to claim damages for false statements made negligently as opposed to fraudulently. This strengthened the buyer's position considerably, as fraud is very difficult to prove. It also provided for the buyer to return the goods and regain his money. In such circumstances, the buyer has much stronger rights if the characteristic complained of relates to the term of the contract. A buyer is in a much weaker position if the remark complained of was made in passing or as part of an advertising puff. It is rather difficult to complain precisely of a claim that a product 'gives results'.

The Trade Descriptions Act, 1968, dealt with a number of points. To mark a good at a particular price on a shop shelf is not a term in a contract or even an offer for sale but an invitation to the public to make offers and both the buyer and seller can withdraw from the potential trade until cash changes hands, but this Act did make it a criminal offence to mark a good at a price below that at which it is in fact for sale. The Act also made it a positive obligation, rather than a discretionary power, for the local authority to enforce the provisions of legislation such as the successive Food and Drugs Acts or the Merchandise Marks Act, 1887. As a result the number of prosecutions has greatly increased and no doubt this development reflects current public opinion. The Trade Descriptions Act extended the scope and spirit of the Merchandise Marks Act by covering services as well as goods and it covers every false or misleading statement in an advertisement. Like most legislation, there are problems of definition and interpretation but the purpose and ambition of the Act is clear from Section 1: 'Any person, who in the course of a trade or business, (a) applies a false description to any goods; or (b) supplies, or offers to supply any goods to which a false trade description is applied; shall . . . be guilty of an offence.' The difficulty is that of definition: if a good in a shop is marked as '£1 formerly £2' it could mean this very good, a similar good in the same shop or a similar good in a quite different shop, although it is clear which of these meanings it is hoped that the customer will infer. The decision rule applied is that any previous price quoted must have applied to the good for twenty-eight consecutive days in the previous six months.

The Unsolicited Goods and Services Act, 1971, provides that private persons who receive unsolicited goods and does not agree to acquire them must let the sender recover them within six months, after which they become his property and there are provisions whereby the recipient can shorten this period. A sender who demands payment for unsolicited goods or theatens legal proceedings is committing a crime.

The Fair Trading Act, 1973, did not of itself introduce any new offences but did create new machinery. A watchdog was created, the Director-General of Fair Trading, assisted by his own staff and a Consumer Protection Advisory Council. The Director's main task is to review trade practices that may adversely affect the consumer and also commercial activities involving monopolistic or restrictive practices; he may interest himself in practices which mislead or confuse customers about the goods or the customer's own rights or which subject them to undue pressure or which lead to an inequitable transaction. The Director-General may make recommendations which, after due process of consultation, may then lead to an order from the Secretary of State. In the event of a criminal prosecution, a compensation order may be made on the Civil Court in favour of the customer under the terms of the Criminal Justice Act, 1972. The Fair Trading Act did away with the office known as the Registrar of

Restrictive Trading Agreements and the functions were transferred to the Director-General.

The Supply of Goods (Implied Terms) Act, 1973, effectively banned exemption clauses in consumer sales and put the buyer in a stronger position than hitherto when, for instance, he might have weakened his position in a subsequent Court case by not specifying what was required but just pointing or using a phrase such as 'one of those'. This Act also makes it impossible for trading stamp proprietors to exclude the warranties of title and merchantability implied by the Trading Stamps Act, 1974.

The Unfair Contract Terms Act, 1977, is an attempt to consolidate the attack on exclusion clauses and makes it impossible for a person to devise a contract term so that he is released from his legal obligations with respect to negligence, breach of contract, and so forth, except in so far as the contract term 'satisfies the requirement of reasonableness'. Schedule 2 which relates to 'reasonableness' reflects the tone of modern consumer legislation.

> The matters to which regard is to be had . . . are any of the following which appear to be relevant:
> (a) the strength of the parties relative to each other . . .
> (b) whether the customer received an inducement to agree to the term . . .
> (c) whether the customer knew or ought reasonably to have known of the extent of the term . . .
> (d) whether the term excludes or restricts any relevant liability of some condition is not complied with . . .
> (e) whether the goods were manufactured, processed or adapted to the special order of the customer.

It is a curious mixture of value judgements and drafting provisions that shift the burden of specifying the effectiveness and applicability of the law to the courts.

The Consumer Credit Act, 1974, attempted to consolidate a situation in which consumer credit through the medium of hire-purchase or its variants had previously been treated differently from consumer credit through the medium of a bank loan. The sale/loan distinction was effectively abolished. To the consumer it is a matter of indifference whether he pays for the purchase by instalments or pays in cash with a loan which is itself repayable by instalments and the philosophy of the Act is to subsume the forms of consumer credit into a whole and then reclassify by function. Effective annual percentage rates of interest must be disclosed and all (save local authorities) operating in consumer credit must be licensed. In the field of commercial credit there were reforms relating to security interests in personal property.

It is difficult to be sure that this plethora of legislation will make much difference to the world. Most purchases are of relatively low value compared with all the costs of pursuing the seller. The most effective stimulus to the seller may well be that he wishes the buyer to return to his shop for he is interested normally in maximising a flow of sales over time rather than making just one sale. This holds less true for the expensive purchase or the single sale made in a street market. Further, where sellers have had to change their methods due to this kind of legislation they are likely to light on some new technique which will then in its turn be declared illegal. There is likely to be a cycle of practices, legislation and court decisions against those practices and then further practices just as there already is in monopoly and tax legislation.

The two legal themes running through the whole area are sanctity of contract and a duty to take care. The former is long-established and became potent in the nineteenth century. It is increasingly realised that what two parties have agreed may not be in the public interest and may not even represent the best interests of each party due to the asymmetric distribution of information. The duty to take care is also well established involving cases, for instance, of early railway trains but, unlike sanctity of contract, it seems to be of increasing importance. No doubt these changes in judicial policy reflect widely held social views and, of course, they have a foundation, of which the law makers are doubtless unaware, in the conclusions of neoclassical economics with respect to monopoly and information.

The law has had difficulty separating monopoly, information and consumer protection and that is exactly because they are all, in fact, inter-related.

NOTES

1   Lord Atkin in course of judgement in *Donoghue* v. *Stevenson*.
2   *Searle* v. *Laverick* (1875) LR 9 QB 122.
3   G. Borrie and A. L. Diamond, *The Consumer, Society and the Law* (Harmondsworth: Penguin, 3rd edn, 1973), p. 100.
4   Institute of Economic Affairs, *Hire Purchase in a Free Society* (London: IEA, 1974).

Chapter 6

The Law and Economics of Labour Markets

INTRODUCTION

This chapter is not primarily about industrial relations, which are the problems of conflict resolution between firms on the one hand, which are themselves a coalition of interest groups, and on the other hand some of their employees who represent one of these interest groups. The focus is rather more on the manner on which the law affects the operation of labour markets and vice versa.

There is a preliminary question on the proper role and scope of the law in disputes between employers and employees and indeed the view is quite widespread that the law is an unsuitable mechanism for resolving such conflicts. The contemporary answer to this prior question of the appropriate role of the law will vary from time to time with the ebb and flow of politics and thus so will the exact form of the law and its impact on labour markets.

It is possible for a given action to fall into any of a number of categories. If the employer fails to provide safe working conditions then a worker's injury might lead to an action for breach of contract or to a tort action and there might also be scope for a criminal action if the lapse were in breach of the Factories Acts. There are therefore the usual classification problems all too common to legal matters; these classifications rarely correspond to economic classifications.

Much of the social meaning of the law in these matters depends on the legal sanction in use. It matters a great deal whether any action taken against strikers is in the civil or criminal courts. It is one thing to make strikes illegal and quite a different matter for an employer to seek damages for breach of contract. For all but a few occupations, strike action is not illegal and the high probability of low awards in a civil case combined with the high costs of going to court mean that there are few such cases and so the strike becomes a powerful negotiating technique.

The main topics within labour law are the contract of employment, the role of any collective bargaining and the statutory control of conditions of work; these topics do, of course, sub-divide still further.

The effect of the law is often uncertain in these matters because an 'agreement' is often perceived by at least one of the parties as a stage in the negotiating proces rather than as a final outcome, while a 'custom of the trade' with respect to, say, manning levels may have just as much impact as a contract enforceable in court. Labour markets do show a continuing *tatonnement* of adjustments and also illustrate the key role of information in the determination of prices, because in this context 'information' includes perceptions as to the exchange bargain with respect to money and work that actually lies behind the contract of employment.

In ordinary discourse a contract is simply an agreement between parties; it then becomes an important issue whether a contract of employment (or in older terms a contract of service) is the same as any other contract, say, that between a householder and a plumber (or in older terms a contract of services). It is widely held that there are differences which hinge on the fact that an employee is a human being while a company has neither a body to be kicked or a soul to be damned. This view holds that a contract of employment is different from other kinds of contract in that the common law model of a contract is a voluntary relationship into which the parties freely entered in terms within the general framework of the law.

This approach will hardly bear serious investigation for, of course, the employer may be a company or a private person. The factors which are important in contracts of employment are the same as those found to be important earlier in considering monopoly and consumer protection law. The key issues are the unequal distribution of bargaining power, an intuitive judgement that the results of such bargaining are unlikely to be in the public interest and the effects of sanctity of contract.

Contracts of any kind may be written, oral or even implied, although there is now widespread encouragement to produce written contracts of employment since the Contracts of Employment Act, 1963, which in fact gives a right to a written agreement. If particular behaviour turns out to be not covered by a contract, then the court will supply the missing terms by reference to the customs and practices of the trade. The court tries to perceive the position in which, if an 'officious bystander' had spelled out the missing terms, the parties would have replied testily that that was all well understood. Over time, as the nature of society has changed, labour law has moved slowly from views of feudal obligations and criminal sanctions (in which the employee has property rights in the employee) to a concern with a free exchange of promises between parties. Recently, a further belief has grown up that this latter model which emphasised sanctity of contract was unrealistic, particularly with respect to the equality of the bargaining powers of the parties, and there has been some movement in the granting of property rights in their jobs to employees.

In principle, a market for labour is like any other market in that the market wage will tend towards an equilibrium wage in which all those seeking work at that wage can find employment and all those seeking workers at that wage can find them. If the actual market wage is not an equilibrium wage then the disequilibrium conditions will provoke an adjustment process that will produce equilibrium where, by definition, there are no vacancies and no unemployed in that market.

This bears little correspondence to reality and we must conclude that real world wages are not market-clearing wages. There are at least three reasons for this outcome that are relevant to the present context. One reason why labour markets do not correspond to textbook models is that the latter only use wages and employment as variables. The employer, however, does not only wish to recruit workers for a given wage in a given occupation and workers in their turn do not only seek employers of their occupation. The employers are not simply interested in a skill which they can identify by some such proxy as a paper qualification or union membership but a whole range of other characteristics such as age, sex and reliability. Employees seek not only wages but other characteristics which may be summarised as working conditions. This is more complex than the simple wage-job model and can lead to the coexistence of vacancies and unemployment.

The law may be relevant here in trying to eliminate some forms of discrimination and health and safety at work legislation may tend to make for uniform working conditions.

A further reason why vacancies and unemployment may coexist is that these are reported vacancies and unemployment but the would-be buyers and sellers in the labour market may have mutually inconsistent perceptions of the market in which they operate. The firm may aspire to levels of skill enjoyed by workers who would not consider working for it and workers may seek jobs that would never be offered to them.

Labour markets may also fail to clear because the buyers and sellers may see themselves as operating in a number of sub-markets so that firms will readily substitute one kind of worker for another rather than change the wage. Similarly, workers may change their occupation rather than take a wage cut in their existing occupation.

The fact that markets are interdependent means that no one market can clear unless all other markets clear simultaneously. This becomes a great difficulty when governments seek to intervene in one labour market on a piecemeal basis with, say, minimum wage legislation. Government policies such as the operation of job and skill centres may help market-clearing while others which support certification processes may well do the opposite.

In the era in which the sanctity of contract principle was at the forefront of legal processes, the employment contract was much like any other in that the underlying spirit was one of robust trading in which it was morally sound to uphold the terms of a contract even if one of the parties had been foolish in coming to such an agreement. The economist's model of perfect competition was seen as supportive of this approach as it was interpreted as upholding the market system. The legal and economic modes of thought were connected, as markets cannot really operate without the division of labour and without a contract system.

The sense in which for many years the law supported the idea of a contract where each side was exchanging characteristics other than just hours of work and hourly wages is seen in *Sagar* v. *Ridehalgh* (1931) 1 Ch 310. In this case the court sustained deductions from wages for bad workmanship and it was claimed that that was the form of the contract which would have to be honoured, even if the worker had been unaware of the custom of the trade in this respect.

The employer's obligations are to pay the agreed wages and any other explicit terms of any contract. He is not obliged to provide work, although there are exceptions, such as the provision of work for an employee who gives exclusive services on commission. Such instances are examples of a more general principle that the parties to the contract are obliged not to impede the performance of the contract. The employer will also have statutory obligations relating to safe working conditions, and so forth.

The employee's obligations are to give faithful and honest service, to use reasonable skill in his work and to obey lawful orders and not commit misconduct. *British Syphon Co. Ltd* v. *Homewood* (1956) 2 All ER 897 showed that an employee hired to give advice 'on all technical matters' had to assign a patent to the employer although the work for it was done on his own account. Apart from this kind of matter, the courts have tended to narrow the meaning of 'faithful' service. There arose a rather unusual position after *Lister* v. *Romford Ice & Cold Storage Co. Ltd* (1957) AC 555 which held that if, due to a lack of reasonable skill in his work, an employee's company were successfully sued, then the employee responsible was personally liable for the damages. The majority Lords laid emphasis on operating a sanction against those who breached a worker's duty to take care. In practice, it seems that insurance companies do not attempt to recover damages against workers in these circumstances.

Having seen the manner in which the courts articulate the idea of employers and employees 'trading' to a mutual exchange of 'work' (defined rather widely) and wages, it is necessary to return to the appropriateness of treating a contract of employment as a freely determined bargain to be sustained in courts.

The legal and economic models underlying such an attitude seem to be both unrealistic and inconsistent with widely held judgements. While it may be true that international opera stars can negotiate a fee in an entirely personal manner and that there are other such cases, the rise of collective bargaining means that for most persons it is quite wrong to think of their employment conditions as the outcome of an individual bargain. Their wages and conditions are negotiated for them and not by them so that their only decision is whether to seek employment elsewhere and in many cases there are no or few such opportunities.

PROPERTY RIGHTS IN EMPLOYMENT

One of the features of British industrial relations has long been the small role accorded to the courts compared to that elsewhere. This is because the trade unions have in the past thought of the courts as their opponents because the courts have been generally supportive of 'sanctity of contract' and have been seen at least as supportive of the employers. The unions sought support from Parliament rather than the courts and, indeed, statutes in 1859, 1871, 1875, 1901 and 1913 were all passed to relieve trade unions of obligations which the courts wished to impose upon them. The rise of collective bargaining had diminished the applicability of the notion of an individual contract and in recent years legislation has rather encouraged the extension of collective bargaining in the United Kingdom. The Employment Protection Act, 1975, for instance, gives the government Advisory, Conciliation and Arbitration Service a statutory duty to 'encourage the extension of collective bargaining'.

The sequence of events is thus that the rise of collective bargaining invalidated the idea of the personal contract and also the idea of the personal contract disenchanted the trade union movement with legal processes so the result of these twin developments was that the contract of employment became less and less like any other contract. The legal sanctions open to employers have become increasingly difficult to find so that the role of the law in the employment contract and in market-clearing can now be stated as a problem from the viewpoint of the employer rather than as a solution.

A second reason, apart from the rise of collective bargaining, for the slow collapse of the notion of the individually negotiated contract is that unemployed labour is socially and politically a quite different outcome to unsold stocks of a product. The economic-legal idea was that in an uncleared market there would be supplies that were unsold during the adjustment process. The modern social and political idea is that the system should be designed so that there is no unemployed labour while the wage adjusts. This value judgement that there should be no unemployment is widely held in the United Kingdom and it has reinforced the move away from legal support for the Adam Smith idea of competitive markets and to the consequent legal idea of property rights in employment.

The third reason why the notion of personal bargaining to which both parties must be held is under strong attack is the realisation that the bargaining power of the parties is very unequal—an idea that we have met in earlier problems.

These three reasons have led to the development of property rights in jobs in that it is becoming—or is perceived as becoming—more difficult to dismiss staff. It is becoming more difficult in two senses: it is becoming more expensive in that redundancy schemes are on the increase and firms now face statutory obligations in this respect; and secondly firms are—or at least feel that they are—more likely than before to face successful litigation for unfair dismissal.

What might be said of an *a priori* nature regarding these developments?

First, it should be asserted that these developments are by no means confined to the United Kingdom, although the newspaper reader might well be forgiven for thinking so.

Secondly, the question for the firm is not really that it is costly to dismiss staff. It would be convenient if the problem were so simple. An encouraging aspect for the firm is that it is the same for all its competitors and its real cause for concern is any differential costs between it and its competitors. This consideration identifies for us the exact form of its problem: in respect of redundancy payments, it must time dismissal so that the present value of its production costs, including redundancy payments and allowing for the consequent effects on production revenues, is preferable to that of the present value of any other time-stream of production costs and revenues.

A third feature of any increase in the property rights of employees in their jobs is that the exchange becomes asymmetric in that the employee can determine the date of his leaving the job quite easily but the employer has much more difficulty in doing so. The employee trades a flow of services which he can end at an agreed notice and in effect often at no notice. The employer is purchasing a flow of services with a fairly open-ended commitment. This third feature will call forth one or a number of possible responses.

The firm may seek to escape the uncertainties and risks in the new situation by resorting to sub-contracting in the event of a sudden increase in demand rather than recruiting extra staff. More drastically, the firm may simply let any increase in demand go unmet rather than face a long-run problem of overstaffing. The problem may also be partially resolved by adopting more mechanised methods of production where this is technically possible rather than face these labour problems. The firm is certainly likely to pay far more attention to recruitment techniques, so that if it must maintain a particular staffing level it is at least holding competent staff.

The general effects can be summarised into two categories. Firms will be more reluctant and more careful in taking on new staff so that the effect may be to increase the length of the period of unemployment for the unemployed and firms will find it more difficult to replace incompetent staff with competent staff. In these senses, such legislation is a plot by the unemployed against the employed and a plot by the less skilled at the expense of the more skilled.

A second category of effects is that the firms will adopt ploys to outmanoeuvre the legislation. An example would be that staff will be dismissed just before they have served long enough to acquire redundancy rights and the contracts of temporary staff will be drafted very carefully indeed.

We can summarise the position with the following hypotheses:

1 the effect on the costs of labour and the uncertainty of the firm's future commitments will reduce the supply of job-offers;
2 the reduction in supply will be particularly severe in the short run as firms learn the new rules of the game;
3 there will be a shift in employers' preferences towards temporary staff rather than permanent staff.

Hypotheses analogous to these have already been tested in a similar case with respect to the granting of property rights to tenants over landlords rather than employees over firms.[7] The results were exactly as predicted by neoclassical economics—that is, that this kind of intervention in labour (or housing) markets works in favour of those who already have jobs (housing) and against those who do not and reduces the total supply of jobs (housing).

It is true that competitive markets do not always produce results which accord with social policy, although in a pluralistic modern society there is great difficulty about just what social policy 'should' be. However, when attempts are made to administer a market by legislation then it is likely that there will be all manner of side-effects, some helpful and some harmful, and economics can predict some of these effects quite reasonably.

A further consequence of administering markets is that those operating in the market may simply break the law rather than face the consequences of the administered market. The Low Pay Unit reports indignantly that minimum wage legislation is widely disregarded in the traditionally low-paid occupations such as catering or hairdressing. Its moral outrage may do it credit but it does no credit to its feeling for how markets work.[2]

It is not in the least surprising that those who cannot get other jobs accept employment at illegally low wages if the alternative is unemployment; it is certainly not surprising that such offers are made to them; and it may even be true that the firms could not afford higher offers. In other words, the illegal bargain may be a better 'trade' than any other available. If the market would produce a different result from that which administrators intend, it is only to be expected that there will be all manner of unintended results from restaurants closing down to direct flouting of the rules as well as the hoped-for results in some cases. If a society stands against the operation of the market and pretends that matters are other than they are, then it must expect perverse results. Free markets do indeed produce awkward results but we cannot wish away the forces that make market prices what they are.

The world may be a disappointing place and we have the options of accepting it, of trying to make some radical change in its nature or of *ad hoc* administrative techniques. If we do choose the third alternative, we must not be surprised if others infer that King Canute is alive and well and trying to administer markets.

INCOMES POLICY AND 'TATONNEMENT'

A further role of the law in labour markets is that of prices and incomes policies which have operated in various forms and with different institutions for nearly twenty years in the United Kingdom. These are anti-inflationary devices which attempt to ensure that all wages and salaries rise at a low rate and it is seen to be politically expedient that the way to do this is to make sure that they all rise at the same, or a similar, rate.

Their effectiveness at limiting inflation is not our present concern which is impact on the operation of labour markets. If all money wages are rising at roughly the same rate then there can be no or few changes in relative wages, and thus wages fail to reallocate labour between markets in the manner illustrated in Chapter 1. If any wage rises are in the form of flat rate increases for everybody then the reallocation process is slowed down even further. Flat rate increases also narrow differentials between occupations and cause unease of a political nature, while undermining the role of trade unions which have a much-restricted role during the operation of such a policy. There are great political problems of monitoring and enforcing such a policy, which is an administrative halfway house between free markets and a controlled economy.

One easily predicted effect is that both firms and trade unions adopt tactical devices so that the market does in fact operate while the firms stay within the form of the law as it is drafted. One much-used device is to raise wages by upgrading staff while they do in fact continue with their same job. A further device is more or less bogus productivity deals. Politically powerful unions claim particular exceptions for themselves. The resource costs of monitoring the wage rises of small firms are too great to be borne and these can effectively disregard the legislation.

The general effect of legislation which redistributes property rights in the labour market, of minimum wage legislation and of prices and incomes policies is to slow down the *tatonnement* process. In one sense this may be the objective of legislation aimed at minimising costs and social distress of the market adjustments. It may seem undesirable to slow down market-clearing but this would only hold if it could be assumed that markets would indeed produce optimal prices and so optimal resource use. Neo-classical economics makes it clear that this assumption will not hold. The choice is then between two non-optimal outcomes—cleared markets with sub-optimal resource patterns on the one hand or slowly cleared markets with sub-optimal resource patterns on the other.

Economics does not provide criteria to make such a choice, which is an inherently political decision, but it does at least clarify some of the effects between which we have to choose.

NOTES

1   D. Maclennan, 'The 1974 Rent Act — some short-run supply effects', *Economic Journal*, vol. 88 (June 1978).
2   Low Pay Unit, *Report No. 16* (London: HMSO, 1978).

NATIONAL UNIVERSITY
LIBRARY

Index